World War I Posters

Gary A. Borkan

Schiffer Publishing Ltd®

4880 Lower Valley Road, Atglen, PA 19310 USA

Dedication

To my wife Martha, who has been supportive of my antiquing for so many years.

Library of Congress Cataloging-in-Publication Data

Borkan, Gary A.
World War I posters / Gary A. Borkan.
p. cm.
ISBN 0-7643-1516-1
1. World War, 1914-1918--Posters--Catalogs. 2. War posters--United States--Catalogs. I. Title: World War One posters. III. Title: World War 1 posters.
D522.25.B67 2002
940.4'88973 dc21
2001005739

Designed by Bonnie M. Hensley
Cover design by Bruce M. Waters
Type set in Korinna BT

ISBN: 0-7643-1516-1
Printed in China
1 2 3 4

Published by Schiffer Publishing Ltd.
4880 Lower Valley Road
Atglen, PA 19310
Phone: (610) 593-1777; Fax: (610) 593-2002
E-mail: Schifferbk@aol.com
Please visit our web site catalog at **www.schifferbooks.com**
We are always looking for people to write books on new and related subjects. If you have an idea for a book please contact us at the above address.

This book may be purchased from the publisher.
Include $3.95 for shipping.
Please try your bookstore first.
You may write for a free catalog.

In Europe, Schiffer books are distributed by
Bushwood Books
6 Marksbury Ave.
Kew Gardens
Surrey TW9 4JF England
Phone: 44 (0) 20 8392-8585; Fax: 44 (0) 20 8392-9876
E-mail: Bushwd@aol.com
Free postage in the U.K., Europe; air mail at cost.

Contents

Acknowledgments 4
Introduction 5
The Artists 6
For the Collector 8
Army Recruiting 12
Navy Recruiting 22
Marine Recruiting 31
Air Service Recruiting 41
Other Services Recruiting 43
United States Shipping Board 52
United States Food Administration 59
United States Fuel Administration 75
United States Department of Agriculture and Garden Army 76
First Liberty Loan of 1917 85
Second Liberty Loan of 1917 89
Third Liberty Loan 95
Fourth Liberty Loan 105
Victory Liberty Loan 113
Miscellaneous and Private Loan Posters 120
War Savings Stamps 129
United War Work Campaign 139
American Red Cross 144
Y.M.C.A. 160
Y.W.C.A. 164
Tributes and Relief 169
Library and Books 181
Official War Films 183
Postwar Readjustment 186
Canada 191
Great Britain 201
Australia 223
France 224
Italy 233
Germany 236
Russia 239

Acknowledgments

I am grateful for the assistance of many people in making this book possible. Nicholas Lowry, President of Swann Galleries, generously provided images of many scarce and rare posters that have been sold by his auction gallery in New York City. Photos of several rare and significant posters were provided by Robert Segel. The photography was accomplished with the excellent assistance of Gregory R. Gilman. Photographic equipment was supplied by Schiffer Publishing Company. Josh Michaud provided considerable assistance with writing and proofreading the poster captions. I wish to thank Dan McInnis and Ian Wright of M&W Graphics of New York City for the excellent mounting and restoration of many of the posters from the author's collection featured in this book. Expert advice and encouragement from David Pollack, Nancy and Morris Steinbock, and Richard Cheek are most appreciated. Sinclair Hitchings and Jane Duggan of the Print Department of the Boston Public Library were supportive and helpful throughout my poster research. My editor, Douglas Congdon-Martin, was instrumental throughout the production of this book, and it would not exist without his help. Finally, I thank my wife, Martha, and my son, Daniel, for their continued support and encouragement.

Introduction

The full color pictorial poster originated in the 1890s and quickly assumed an essential role in advertising. Given the proven power of this medium, it was only natural that posters would have a significant role in World War I propaganda. Many of the leading artists and commercial illustrators of the age designed posters for their country's war effort. These artists had the experience and skill to produce bold and effective large graphics that could be absorbed at a single glance. Many of these posters were printed with the wonderfully lush process of color lithography and were striking works of commercial art. Because of their beauty and, often, a sense of national pride, many of these posters were saved and preserved. They still are being found today stored away in homes and institutions after nearly a century.

World War I posters can tell us much about the history of the war, the requirements of the war effort, and the spirit of the citizenry in the era. These posters represent a period of history now passed from the living memory of all but a very few people. However, the posters still convey the passion, power, and patriotism they were intended to express. They speak to us still, and are therefore enthusiastically appreciated and collected today.

The purpose of this book is to introduce the posters of World War I and to provide some background to their history, production, artists, and subject matter. It will also demonstrate the wide range of war posters produced, showing not only the greatest works, but also the many text-only posters that made up a large part of the production. The emphasis is on American posters, but a substantial number of Canadian, British, French, and other European works are also included.

The Poster Campaign in the United States in World War I

The United States government created the Committee of Public Information within a week of declaring war with Germany. The director was George Creel, editor of the Rocky Mountain News in Denver. The Committee ultimately engaged the services of hundreds of writers, artists, and speakers to promote the war effort. Creel later wrote, "In all things, without halt or change, it was a plain publicity proposition, a vast enterprise in salesmanship, the world's greatest adventure in advertising."

At the same time the Committee of Public Information was being formed, the Society of Illustrators met in New York City to discuss ways in which American artists could contribute to the war effort. During one of these meetings the President of the Society, Charles Dana Gibson received a telegram from Creel requesting aid in producing artworks for the war. Gibson later commented that the telegram was perfectly timed, interrupting a long discussion over how artists might become involved. The telegram explained exactly how they could begin to participate in the war effort.

On April 22, Gibson met with Creel and together they formed the Division of Pictorial Publicity of the Committee of Public Information. Gibson was appointed head of the new Division, an excellent choice based on his reputation, popularity and personality. He chose as his Vice Chairman, Frank De Sales Casey, who was Art Director at Collier's Magazine. Together these two men successfully recruited many of America's most famous fine and commercial artists to the war effort. Brief biographies of some of the most important artists are given later in this book.

Gibson described the operations of the Division in producing posters, "We have a meeting every Friday night. This takes place at our headquarters, 200 Fifth Avenue, where we meet men who are sent to us with their requests by the different departments in Washington. Suppose we have with us someone from the Food Administrator's Office, sent to us so that we can get more clearly in mind the needs of his division through personal contact. Casey, once having got the suggestion, picks out two of the best men he thinks can be found for the work... In the course of dinner views are exchanged on all sides, and we come to understand each other pretty thoroughly."

Each week Casey traveled to Washington with sketches and drawings for approval by government agencies. In developing designs with the artists, Gibson repeatedly stressed that posters should reflect ideas rather than specific events. This was a challenge for many of the illustrators, who were used to portraying detailed scenes in magazine stories and books.

In the twenty months of its existence between April 1917 and November 1918, the Division of Pictorial Publicity submitted 700 poster designs to 58 government departments. It produced hundreds of additional trolley and bus cardboard posters, and hundreds of advertisements, cartoons, and banners. None of the artists were paid for their work, though they had been used to receiving hundreds or thousands of dollars for a single commercial or fine artwork.

The Art of the Poster leading up to World War I

The modern poster originated around 1890 in France, coinciding with the Art Nouveau movement. Jules Cheret is typically credited with being the first to fully exploit and elaborate this medium. Before this time posters were primarily printed text, although they often used multiple type faces and different colors within the individual poster. Pictures were rarely utilized, and were generally small within the overall composition of text.

Cheret's innovation was to expand the size of the poster and use color lithography in three or four colors to make a very bold graphic statement. The image frequently occupied the full sheet and the advertising was placed within and around the image. The picture and text could be absorbed simultaneously with a single glance and understood from a distance.

The Art Nouveau style flourished throughout the 1890s, featuring sinuous and sensual floral and pictorial designs, and beautiful ladies were a favorite subject. Among the leading poster artists were the great Toulouse-Lautrec and Mucha. The public became fascinated with poster art, and posters proved fabulously effective and popular. During the next 20 years, poster art became pervasive throughout Europe and America.

The modernistic American posters of the 1890s primarily advertised the magazine and book publishing industry and were typically small. These posters were not directed to a mass audience but rather the educated and adventurous intellectual. However, by 1900, boldly colorful vaudeville, circus, and other theatrical posters were all over the walls of American cities and towns. Product advertising posters were less prevalent in the United States than in Europe, though there were vast numbers of poster-like product advertisements in popular magazines. In the United States, poster design was the province of skilled craftsmen who produced vibrant and effective works, but rarely even signed their names. Their posters were rarely what would be considered fine art or inventive for the era.

The American artists who were recruited to design posters for the World War I effort were the country's most famous illustrators. Few had much experience designing posters. Their primary occupation had been to illustrate magazine stories, books, and magazine covers. In this era, magazine illustrations were usually quite detailed and specific, they had little to do with modern poster design. On the other hand, magazine covers were much like miniature posters in their look, style, and purpose. It was through bold and creative covers that early 20th Century magazines vied for attention on the newsstand. Thus the illustrator's considerable experience in producing magazine covers gave them a great head start in understanding poster design.

Indeed, when we compare early 1900s theatrical posters with the World War I posters, we see an interesting contrast. In the earlier posters there was a wonderful use of color and imagery, but they had a straightforwardness and similarity of style that was charming but not exciting. When the artists in the Division of Pictorial Publicity designed war posters, they proved their reputations by producing a great range of posters in many different styles. The sameness of the pre-war posters is gone. World War I American posters show considerable variety, yet are consistently effective as posters. This may also be attributable to the structure of the Division in overseeing the poster designs and to the cooperation between the artists.

The Artists

Among the hundreds of accomplished artists who designed World War I posters, a few deserve special mention (alphabetically)

Frank Brangwyn (1867-1956) was an important English fine artist and designer in many fields; he first worked for William Morris. He was a leading war artist and many of his black and white lithographs for newspapers were published as posters.

Charles Livingston Bull (1874-1932) was a noted magazine and book illustrator whose specialty was animals. He designed two very fine posters, *Keep him free* and *Join the Army Air Service.*

Howard Chandler Christy (1873-1952) was one of the leading illustrators before the war. He was famed for his "Christy Girls," typically lovely society girls in elegant settings. His work included some of the most famous war posters including *I wish I were a man...* and other fine recruiting and bond posters.

Harrison Fisher (1875-1934) was a popular American magazine and book illustrator. He designed only a few fine World War I posters. The best is *I summon you to the comradeship.*

James Montgomery Flagg (1877-1960) was an immensely successful commercial and fine artist before and after the war. He designed some of the very greatest war posters, his most famous being *I want you* featuring Uncle Sam.

Charles Dana Gibson (1867-1944) was famed for his black and white ink drawings of lovely girls in high society, known as "Gibson Girls." These appeared in Life Magazine primarily and in numerous books of his works. He was chairman of the Division of Pictorial Publicity during the war and spearheaded the American poster effort. He actually designed very few posters.

Ludwig Hohlwein (1874-1949) was one of Germany's most successful and prolific poster artists throughout the early 20th century. He designed many important German World War I posters.

Lucien Jonas (1880-1947) was a noted French illustrator and lithographer. He produced fine French World War I posters, and several for the American war effort.

Joseph Christian (J. C.) Leyendecker (1874-1951) was a leading cover artist for the Saturday Evening Post for over 25 years, and created important advertising art including the "Arrow Collar Man." He designed several war posters, among them the famous Boy Scout image for Fourth Liberty Loan.

Neysa Moran McMein (1890-1949) was a popular and glamorous woman illustrator who produced many McCall's covers. She produced several World War I posters, including a lovely nurse poster for Y.M.C.A.

Herbert Paus (1880-1946) was a well-regarded illustrator who is most known for his many World War I posters. He was one of the more prolific of the World War I poster artists.

Edward Penfield (1866-1925) was one of America's most innovative and modern posterists in the 1890s. He went on to a leading career in illustration and cover art. His few war posters are scarce and highly prized. The most famous shows women of France pulling a plow.

Joseph Pennell (1860-1922) was an extremely well-regarded fine art lithographer and illustrator. Pennell wrote important books on art and a biography of James M. Whistler. He designed the famous Fourth Liberty Loan poster showing an air raid on the Statue of Liberty and wrote a book about its production.

Louis Raemaekers (1869-1956) was a prolific fine artist and lithographer, best known for satirical and political cartoons in United States and abroad. He produced several war posters and books of war illustrations.

Henry Reuterdahl (1871-1925) specialized in nautical painting and produced many fine Navy-related World War I posters.

Adolph Triedler (1886-?) was a poster artist and illustrator with a very long career. He produced notable posters in both World War I and II, and some fine travel posters.

For the Collector

Poster Printing Techniques

Probably 90 percent of World War I posters were printed by color lithography, also known as chromolithography. This printing technique produced very rich coloration, which accounts for a considerable part of the appeal of these posters when we see them today.

Color lithography was little used for poster work after the 1930s and is very labor-intensive to reproduce today. Poster collectors and dealers become familiar with the look of a true color lithograph and can differentiate it from the more prevalent modern halftone process printing. Then it becomes much easier to tell real from reproduction war posters.

The lithographic process begins with a specially prepared stone or zinc plate. The artist draws the image on the stone (plate) with a greasy crayon. When chemically treated, the portion of the plate with the drawing holds and transfers the ink to the paper, whereas the blank portion does not hold or transfer any ink. Black and white printing uses only a single lithographic stone and black ink.

In color lithography, the design of the original artwork is separated by the skilled lithographic artist into different printing plates, one for each color to be used. Only those portions of the image pertinent to that color are drawn on each plate. If the individual plates are properly inked and printed successively in perfect registration, a full color lithograph print results. This process does not typically blend or overlap colors on the paper to form other colors. Thus, quite a large number of lithographic stones with specific colors and shades may be needed. Elaborate color lithographs may employ 8 to 20 or more different plates for completion, and each plate is inked and printed separately. Color lithography is a very skilled and labor-intensive process, and this accounts for the decline in its use, except in the field of fine artist work today.

Halftone process printing, which was perfected in the 1890s, prints in full color using three colors (cyan, magenta, yellow) or four colors (adding black). This method requires photographing the subject (original artwork) through a series of color filters and mesh screens, to separate the image into its primary colors. The printing plates thus produced have tiny dots of varying sizes which determine the intensity and distribution of that particular color. When properly prepared, these halftone plates print a full color image with fine gradations of tones. In the halftone process the colors appear to the eye to blend to make all the other colors. The great strength of this process is that it reproduces all colors and tonal ranges.

Although it takes experience and familiarity with antique prints and posters to know what true lithography looks like, a few pointers may be suggested. There are multiple varieties and styles of color lithographs, but most often it will be seen that the piece looks convincingly like an original crayon or pastel drawing on the paper. Indeed, it is often hard to tell a color lithograph from a hand drawn original. The other typically seen type of color lithograph displays masses of solid colors with no white spaces or dots within the color areas.

The halftone process is much easier to identify. Under magnification one sees an evenly spaced grid of dots (though the dots may be of varying sizes). Usually four basic colors (cyan, magenta, yellow, black) comprise these dots and there are white spaces between the dots. Look at the pictures in this book under 5 or 10 power magnification and you will become familiar with the dot-matrix appearance of the halftone process print. You will see the same appearance in any popular color printing. Because of the white spaces between the color dots of halftone process printing, these prints often do not have the intensity that characterizes color lithography. That is why the original posters are often noted to have such rich and intense colors, whereas reproductions often appear "washed out".

It should be mentioned that a substantial number of perfectly genuine World War I posters were printed by the halftone process, and these will be noted in the captions of the photos in this book.

Preservation of World War I Posters

Not surprisingly, World War I posters can vary hugely in condition. Many have come through the years badly damaged, yet others may be virtually in mint original condition.

Frequently groups of World War I posters are found rolled together. The posters on the outside of the roll may show severe effects of aging, whereas ones inside may be near mint. This is especially true if narrower posters are rolled inside of wider ones, as commonly occurred. Then even the edges of the smaller posters may be choice. Typically smaller posters survive in better condition than larger ones and are more likely to be found in near mint condition.

World War I poster paper was thin and tears very easily, yet it is rarely brittle even today. Folds in the paper can often be unfolded and flattened. Posters don't usually shatter from brittleness as newsprint from the era would. However, some of the war posters were on a low grade wood pulp paper much like newsprint. These are frequently found torn, damaged, or very brittle. Fortunately these were a minority of the posters produced.

Grading and Condition

Like any collectible, the condition of an antique poster has a great effect on its value. Condition grading in the poster field is not as officially standardized as in such fields as coin collecting. However, it has become acceptable to differentiate by letter grade with the following conventions:

Condition A designates a poster in excellent condition. The colors are fresh, there are no more than a couple tiny margin-only tears, no paper loss, and folds or wrinkles if any should be nearly invisible. If the poster is just as printed with no flaws whatever, it may be termed "mint" or A+.

Condition B designates a poster in good condition. There may be very slight fading or faint stain. If there is minor restoration, it is not immediately apparent. There may be a number of tears, none over several inches long, and only a tiny amount of paper loss.

Condition C designates a poster in fair condition. Moderate fading or staining may be seen. Restoration and folds may be quite pronounced, there may be some flaking of paper or minor paper loss.

Among the various condition problems which may be encountered in old posters several are more serious than others. The most critical flaws are when the poster is laminated or varnished on its surface or pasted irreversibly to an improper backing which may cause degradation of the paper. When a poster has been exposed to light, heat, or air for a long period, serious fading, brittleness and browning of paper occurs. When the colors are badly impaired this greatly affects value. Staining from grease, paint, or ink are very serious and often cannot be reversed. Large tears and large paper losses are very serious, although small tears or slight losses in the margins only are less critical for the collector. As with any collectable, the value of a poster varies hugely between excellent and poor condition.

Conservation and Restoration

There are number of considerations for preservation and display of antique posters. The first decision is whether to keep the poster unmounted or have it archivally "linen" mounted. For posters of one-sheet or smaller size in excellent condition, such mounting may not be necessary. Larger posters may need mounting for support, and damaged posters are best restored through the linen mounting process. Many poster dealers typically mount all posters as a matter of course for ease of their display at shows or galleries.

The archival mounting used in the poster field is commonly termed linen mounting yet the fabric used is actually cotton canvas. The canvas has a layer of acid-free paper pasted on it, upon which the poster is glued with rice paste. This process should "not be tried at home" as the saying goes. It must be performed by specialists with experience, equipment, space, and proper materials. Results by professionals can be quite remarkable. Tears lay down neatly and in some cases nearly disappear entirely. Once the poster is mounted, missing portions can be pieced-in with similar old poster paper. Touch-up or even recreation of missing portions with colored pencils or watercolor can achieve remarkable results.

Linen mounting, if done properly, enhances the value and desirability of a vintage poster for a large majority of serious collectors and dealers. The process of linen backing is archival and fully reversible, the poster can easily be removed by professionals should the need arise. There is a smaller number of collectors who prefer unmounted posters. They may be concerned about any modification of the original antique or about not being able to see the original condition of the poster before mounting.

For posters that do not need mounting yet have very minor flaws, some conservative repairs may be attempted by the experienced collector or dealer. For posters with small tears, repairs can be made from the back with archival paper tape such as Filmoplast P-90 or similar products. Small patches of archival paper or old similar poster paper can applied with archival wheat paste. Patches and archival tape should be as small and limited as possible to accomplish the repair. Minor touch-up with colored pencil or delicate watercolor can also be done to restore the image. Permanent markers or paint must not be used.

Certain "restoration" practices must strenuously be avoided. It should be obvious that no tape can be on the front of the image. Cellophane tape must not be used (especially the clear shiny type which will discolor the paper within a couple years). Masking tape will also discolor the paper in a few years and these discolorations cannot be reversed. Rubber cement is equally bad and will stain the paper permanently. Never use hot melt glue either!

Any type of drymounting on matboard, foamcore, or any other material should also be avoided. This frequently cannot be reversed. Quite frequently the poster is laid down unevenly and permanent creases are introduced. Drymounting will nearly destroy the resale value of any antique poster and many poster dealers will not buy drymounted posters.

Unfortunately, frame shops strongly encourage drymounting because it gives a very flat product for the purchaser. It may be hard to resist the desperate pleas of the frame shop proprietor to drymount the poster. The poster collector should accept a few ripples as evidence of the ephemeral nature of the artwork. To the serious enthusiast, these irregularities add to the charm and eye appeal of the poster.

Framing and Display

Because they tear so easily, unmounted posters cannot be displayed or shown "loose" without sustaining serious damage. Furthermore, when paper is exposed to the atmosphere it ages very rapidly, air is perhaps the worst enemy of antique paper! Under no circumstances should a poster be displayed on a wall without protective covering for more than a short time. Within a year an uncovered poster would experience the same aging that would take many years if framed or wrapped.

Posters can be framed using proper industry techniques. Metal or wood frames are satisfactory. Glass or Plexiglass are acceptable, non-UV is preferable. The poster should be matted, or at least spaced away from the glass if possible. Backing boards should be archival and the poster may hinged at the top if needed. The poster should never be glued or taped with double sided tape to the backing board.

Dealers or collectors may wish to have their posters shrink wrapped on foamcore or corrugated cardboard for display. This takes less space and may preserve them from air exposure or damage. Shrink film will not harm the poster, but a shrink-wrapped poster should probably be rewrapped with new backing within 5 years or so. Corrugated cardboard will introduce discoloration if used as a backing for longer than this interval.

Once the poster is framed or wrapped, care must be taken in display. Sunlight and heat must be avoided. If the poster is exposed to sunlight it will fade rapidly and this cannot be reversed. Even with UV filtering glass, it would be unwise to leave a framed poster in bright light. Putting it near a radiator is equally dangerous because heat accelerates the aging process.

Desirability, Rarity, and Value of World War I Posters

Many factors contribute to the value of a World War poster. These include the popularity of the artist and the particular image, as well as the subject, condition, and rarity. As you examine the photographs in this book with their associated value ranges, you will begin to get a sense of this price structure in this field.

Generally, recruiting posters for the major military services are the most sought after. Since there were very few posters made for the Air Service, Mounted Cavalry, and Tank Corps, these are the most valuable. Posters recruiting men for the Marines, Army, and Navy are very popular, but more varieties were produced and their values are slightly less. Smaller services such as Medical Corps, Merchant Marines, and others produced few designs and these are scarce and desirable.

Posters for the many home front campaigns and causes tend to be less costly. There were numerous great posters produced for the Liberty Loans, War Savings Stamps, American Red Cross, Y.M.C.A., Y.W.C.A., and dozens of other organizations. For reasons not entirely clear, when groups of war posters are found, these are the posters that typically turn up and recruiting posters remain scarce.

Among the artists who produced war posters, James Montgomery Flagg and Howard Chandler Christy may be most famous and highly regarded. Both produced some of the greatest recruiting posters of the war and some very fine home front posters, especially for bonds. As will be seen in the photo section, their prices range widely, with recruiting posters being much more valuable than the bond posters. Also their recruiting posters are many times rarer than their bond posters.

Less valuable posters include many pieces which have only text or are primarily text with only a small image. These may actually be very scarce and provide an important window on the range of efforts in World War I publicity. This book includes images of a number of these posters, many of which may not have been published before. Because they are not as decorative, many of these posters were not saved or have been thrown away in intervening years. Nevertheless, when found they are much less expensive than larger pictorial posters.

Although most World War I posters that will be found are for national recruiting or national home front campaigns, there were hundreds and perhaps thousands of regional or local posters produced during the war. Some are illustrated in this book. These tend to clearly identify the region they originate from and their local nature is apparent from the text of the poster. They seldom were done by the leading artists, though there are exceptions. These posters tend to be scarce, but are not in as great demand as the national issues. Thus they may be more reasonably priced than their actual rarity would suggest.

Generally speaking, one-sheet posters (approximately 30" x 40") tend to be more valuable than half-sheets (typically 20" x 30"). A limited number of posters in the two-sheet size were made. They are quite impressive, but may be too big for some collectors. Still these are more valuable as a rule and are uncommon in nice condition. Small posters, below half-sheet size, may be lower priced, since they typically are not as dramatic or impressive.

Certain American posters may be highlighted as being among the most prized and these are all extremely scarce to rare:

James Montgomery Flagg: *I want you for U. S. Army*
James Montgomery Flagg: *Columbia calls*
James Montgomery Flagg: *Wake up America*
Howard Chandler Christy: *I wish I were a man*

Angiet Hutaf: *Treat 'em rough, join the Tanks*
Fred Spear: *Enlist* ("Lusitania")
Coles Phillips: *Light consumes coal*
L. N. Britten: *Warning* (sinking Biplane)
H. R. Hopps: *Help stop this* ("King Kong")
Charles Livingston Bull: *Join the Army Air Service*

Reproductions

Ten or more years ago, very few World War I posters had been reproduced. Today on the internet, numerous war poster reproductions are available from many suppliers. While in the past it was an expensive undertaking to reproduce a poster, now printing is frequently done overseas at low cost, and much more limited production runs are possible with newer techniques. However, if a collector is familiar with the appearance and size of the original posters, these reproductions are unlikely to present significant problems in identification.

Typically, when a poster is reproduced it is done using the halftone process based on photographing an original poster. The resulting image is very different from the color lithography that characterized perhaps 90 percent of original World War I posters. As indicated earlier, the halftone process uses four colors and under magnification tiny dots of these colors are very apparent. This is exactly the same type of printing used in any magazine or book (including this one). Color lithographs have solid areas of color, or the appearance of crayon or pastel drawing under magnification. It would reward the collector of antique posters to look at known antique specimens under magnification, and more importantly to look at modern halftone process prints under magnification. Today, there are also various inkjet and laser printing techniques, and some of these printers can produce impressive large reproduction posters. These modern copies under magnification may look different from halftone process prints, but they also look quite different from the color lithograph originals.

The size of reproduction posters is also almost invariably different from the originals. Check the size of posters in this book; this can be a very important authentication tool. Very few of the original posters were made in more than one size, those that were have been noted in the captions. If the real poster is 30" x 40", then a poster in size 23" x 32", for example, is very suspicious. One should of course make allowance for the possibility that the poster under consideration has had margins trimmed, as may occur in posters that have been restored or linen mounted and are still completely authentic.

Another important tool is familiarity with the paper used in World War I posters. The paper of antique World War I posters is very different from that used for reproductions, but knowledge of this comes with handling the originals. It should be noted that World War I posters found on shiny thin bright white paper are suspect. One of the most surprising and telltale flaws seen in reproduction posters may occur when a damaged original poster is used as the basis for the photographic reproduction. Typically any post-printing flaws in the original such at tears, repairs, tape, discoloration are actually printed into the reproduced image. This is invariably a sign of a reproduction, and is useful to bear in mind when considering all types of antique paper items.

As with any type of collectible, one cannot hope to recognize reproductions without having seen a substantial number of originals. Once one is familiar with authentic World War I posters, reproductions are not much of a problem, and will be unlikely to prove a significant problem in the near future either. Fortunately, World War I poster reproductions are not usually deceptive to the collector or dealer with even moderate levels of experience.

Interpreting the Photograph Captions

The photograph captions use the following format: title, artist, size, publishing agency, printing company, location of printer, and price range. The source of image follows the poster caption, if no source given the poster is in the author's collection.

The price ranges in this book reflect retail selling prices, wholesale values would be less. The range may be viewed as reflecting "B" condition for the lower price given, and "A" condition for the higher price. Perfect mint specimens or mint specimens that are linen mounted may sell even higher. On the other hand, a specimen with significant staining, fading, large paper loss, severe tears or improper mounting is worth far less than the lower estimate. A damaged and flawed poster is worth much less than 50 percent of the low figure given. Even at a very low price a significantly flawed poster may be difficult to sell.

As any collector who goes to antique shows, shops, or auctions is aware, prices for a given collectible can vary wildly. This is especially true in live or internet auctions where "auction fever" can yield a surprisingly high price on an item, or the absence of any serious buyers can lead to a very low price. The prices in this book have been chosen to indicate the center of the range for each item, reflecting relative desirability, scarcity and previous price records.

Army Recruiting

Men wanted for the army, I. B. Hazelton, 30" x 40", U. S. Army, no printer. $400-$550.

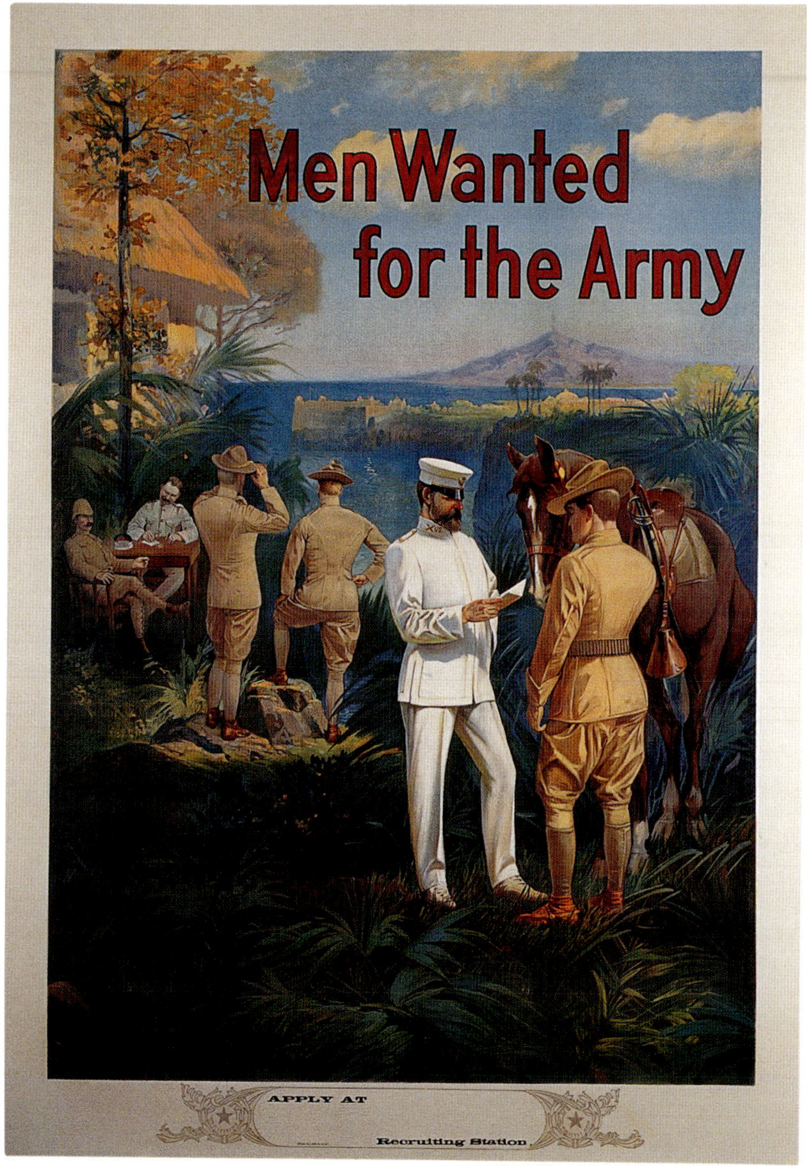

Men wanted for the army, I. B. Hazelton, 30" x 40", U. S. Army, no printer. $400-$550.

Men wanted for the army, I. B. Hazelton, 30" x 40", U. S. Army, no printer. $400-$550.

Men wanted for the army, I. B. Hazelton, 30" x 40", U. S. Army, no printer. $900-$1200. Most desirable of this prewar series of four posters, showing mounted cavalry officer.

Enlist, Fred Spear, 30" x 40", Boston Committee of Public Safety, no printer. This also exists in a 23" x 32" format. $7000-$9000. Both sizes are very rare and extremely desirable. *Courtesy of Swann Galleries.*

The minute men of to-day are going to Plattsburg, unsigned, 20" x 27", Military Training Camps Association, no printer. $300-$450.

Are you trained to defend your country? Plattsburg, unsigned, 20" x 27", Military Training Camps Association, no printer. $300-$450.

Are you trained to do your share? Plattsburg, unsigned, 20" x 27", Military Training Camps Association, no printer. $300-$450.

I want you for U. S. Army, James Montgomery Flagg, 30" x 40", U. S. Army, Leslie Judge, New York. $3000-$4500. The most popular WWI poster and very scarce, perhaps the most famous poster ever issued! *Courtesy of Swann Galleries.*

Destroy this mad brute, H. R. Hopps, 28" x 41", U. S. Army, Traung Label and Lithograph Co. $8000-$10000. Remarkable 1916 poster predating American involvement, extremely rare and popular. *Courtesy of Swann Galleries.*

Our regular divisions, James Montgomery Flagg, 20.5" x 28", U. S. Army, Sackett and Wilhelms, Brooklyn. $600-$750. *Courtesy of Swann Galleries.*

First Division, Otho Cushing, 19" x 25", U. S. Army, Engineer Reproduction Plant, Washington D.C. $300-$450.

Wanted! 500 bakers for the U. S. Army, Dewey, 28.5" x 40.5", U. S. Army, National Printing and Engraving, New York, $600-$750. *Courtesy of Swann Galleries.*

Enlist to-day in the 69th Infantry, unsigned, 28.5" x 40.5", U. S. Army, Empire City Job Print, New York. $500-$650. Scarce poster promoting Irish-American Regiment.

Pro Patria! Join Army for period of war, Welsh, 28" x 42", U. S. Army, Hegeman Print, New York. $400-$550.

The call to duty, unsigned, 30" x 40.5", Recruiting Committee of the Mayor's Committee on National Defense, American Litho Co., New York. $400-$550.

Columbia calls, Frances Adams Halstead, 30" x 40", U. S. Army, no printer. $300-$450.

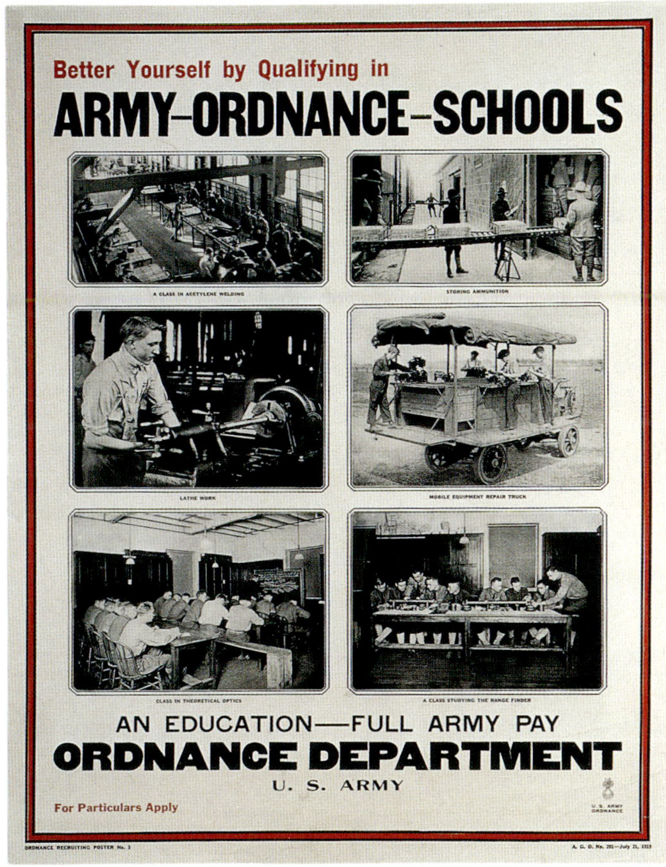

Army-Ordnance Schools, unsigned, 19" x 25", Ordnance Department, A.G.O. No. 201, July 21, 1919. $300-$450.

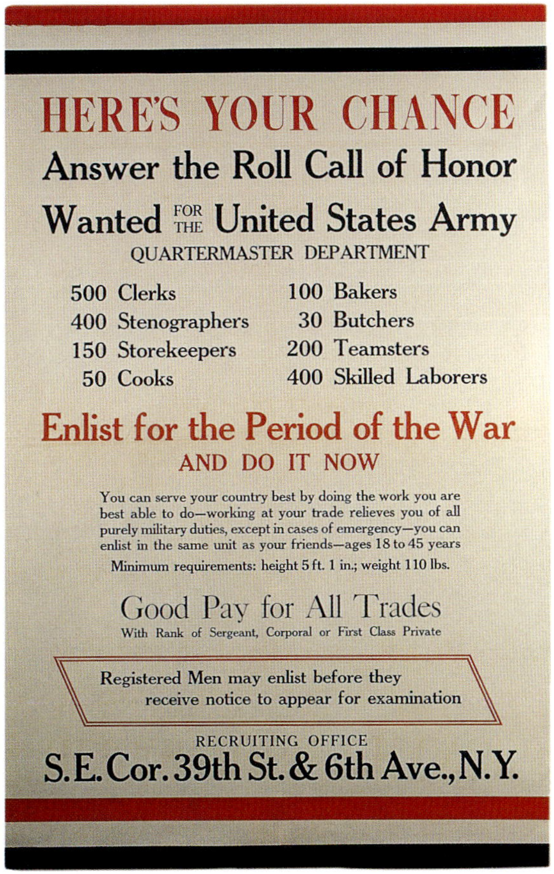

Here's your chance, unsigned, 25" x 41", United States Army, Quartermaster Corps, no printer. $100-$150.

Learn to make and test the big guns, C. B. Falls, 19" x 25", Ordnance Dept. Engineer Reproduction Plant, U. S. Army, Washington D. C. $300-$450.

Wanted 300,000 volunteers for U. S. Army, unsigned, 22" x 32", U. S. Army, no printer. $200-$300. Unusual double-sided poster, scarce.

Stop! Look! Listen! Enlist now, unsigned, 22" x 32", U. S. Army, no printer. The reverse of the double-sided poster. $200-$300.

Navy Recruiting

Here he is, Sir, Charles Dana Gibson, 28" x 42", U. S. Navy, Latham Litho, Brooklyn, New York. $600-$750. One of Gibson's few war posters, perhaps his best.

The Navy needs you! Don't read American history- make it!, James Montgomery Flagg, 28" x 42", U. S. Navy, no printer. $600-$750.

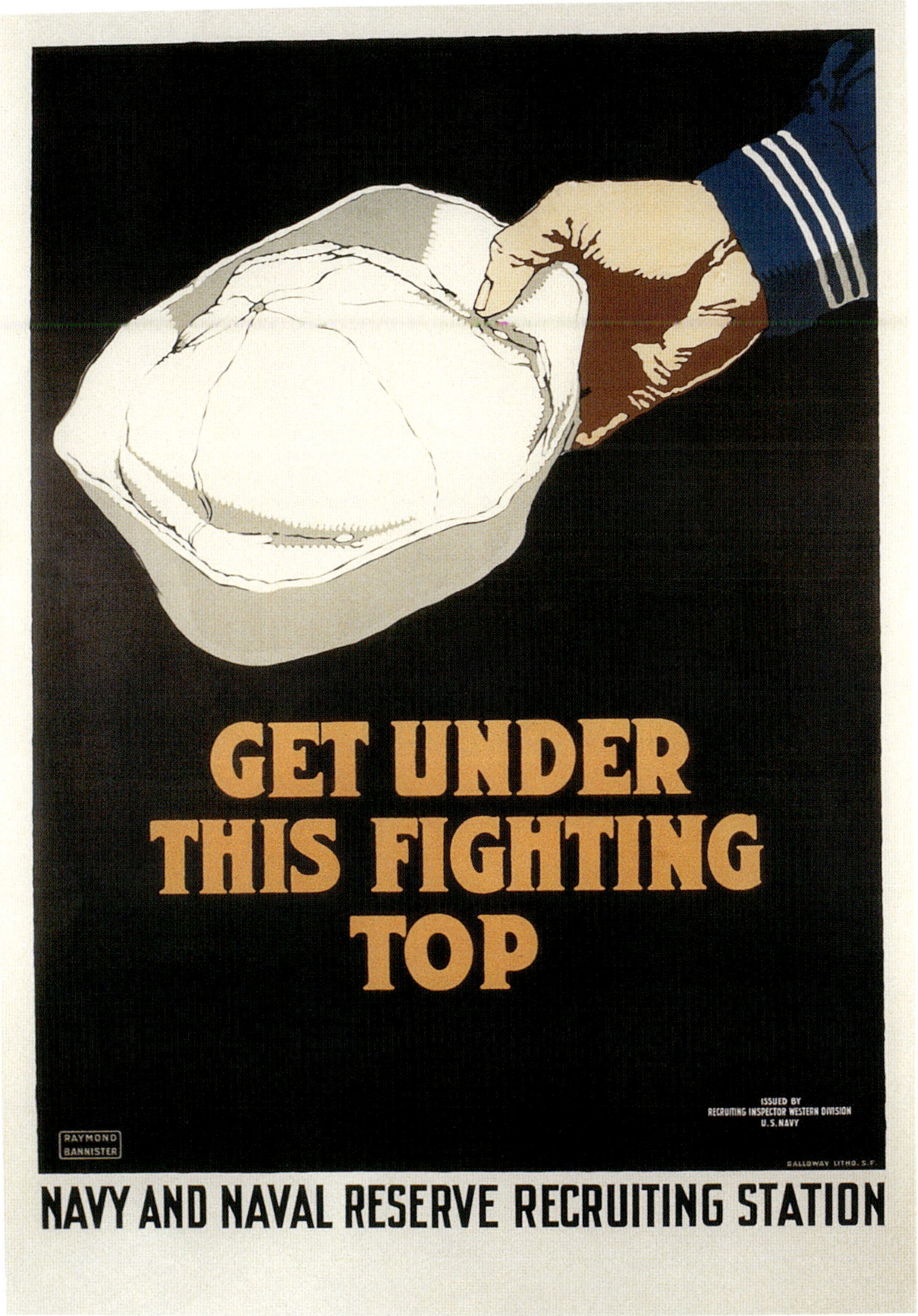

Get under this fighting top, Raymond Bannister, 28" x 42", U. S. Navy, Galloway Litho, San Francisco. $500-$650. *Courtesy of Swann Galleries.*

Join the Navy, the service for fighting men, R. F. Babcock, 28" x 42", U. S. Navy, no printer. $500-$650. *Courtesy of Swann Galleries.*

I want you for the Navy, Howard Chandler Christy, 27" x 41.5", U. S. Navy, Forbes, Boston. $900-$1200. *Courtesy of Swann Galleries.*

Gee!! I wish I were a man, I'd join the Navy, Howard Chandler Christy, 27" x 41", U. S. Navy, no printer. $1500-$2000. *Courtesy of Swann Galleries.*

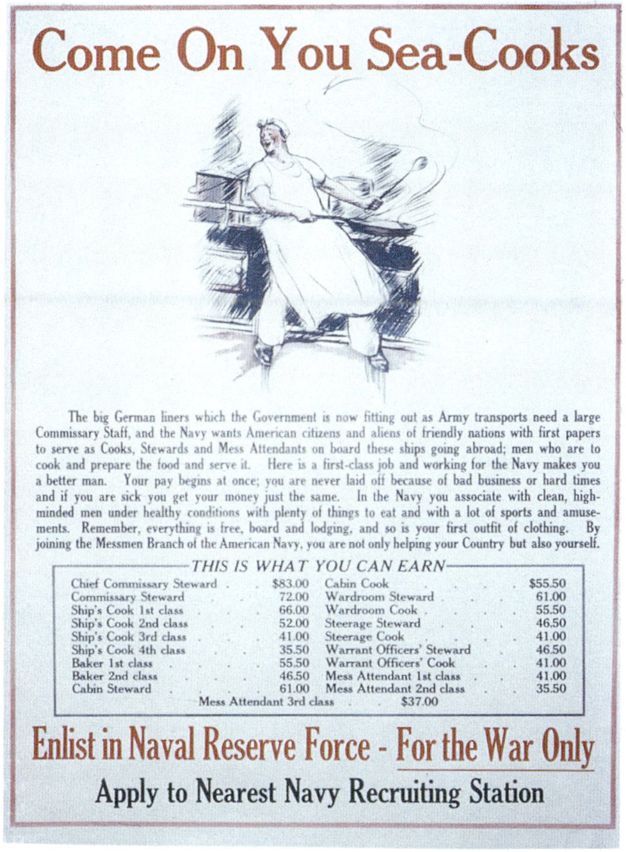

Come on you sea-cooks, Wallace Morgan, 21" x 28", Naval Reserve, U. S. Navy, no printer. $300-$450. *Courtesy of Swann Galleries.*

The Navy needs you, unsigned, 25" x 40.5", U. S. Navy, Press of Howe Addressing Co., Philadelphia. $200-$300.

The Navy is calling, L. N. Britten, 28" x 41", U. S. Navy, W. F. Powers Co., New York. $400-$550.

The Navy put 'em across, H. Reuterdahl, 28" x 45", Press U. S. Navy Recruiting Bureau. $400-$550.

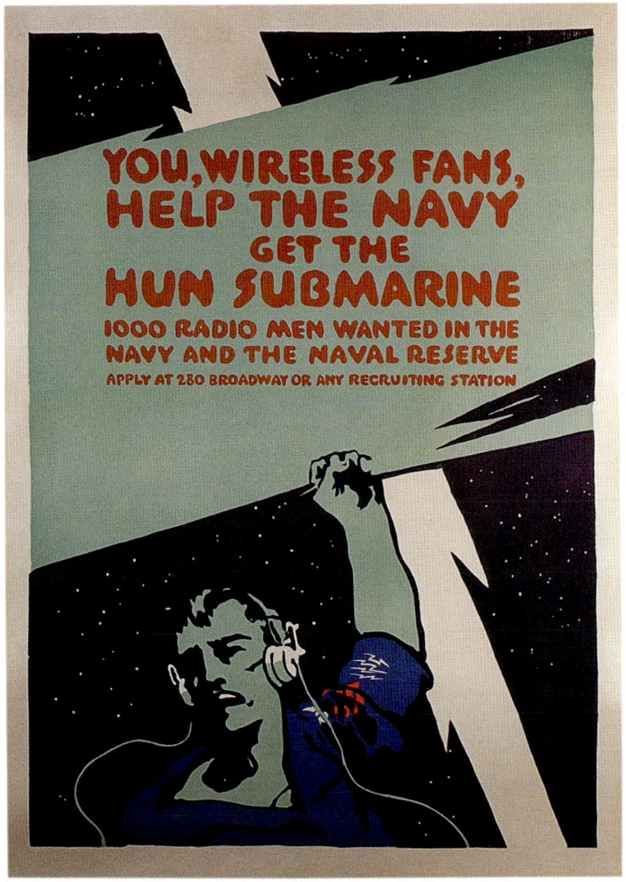

You, wireless fans, help the Navy get the Hun submarine, C. B. Falls, 28" x 40", U. S. Navy, no printer. $500-$650. Scarce wireless related poster.

Your navy calls for 2,000 firemen, Harold von Schmidt, 28" x 41" U. S. Navy, Francis-Valentine Print Co., San Francisco. $400-$550. Scarce fire-related theme.

Help deliver the goods, Herbert Paus, 28" x 41", U. S. Navy American Litho Co., New York. $400-$550.

The sword is drawn the Navy upholds it!, Kenyon Cox, 28" x 42", U. S. Navy, H. C. Miner Co. $500-$650.

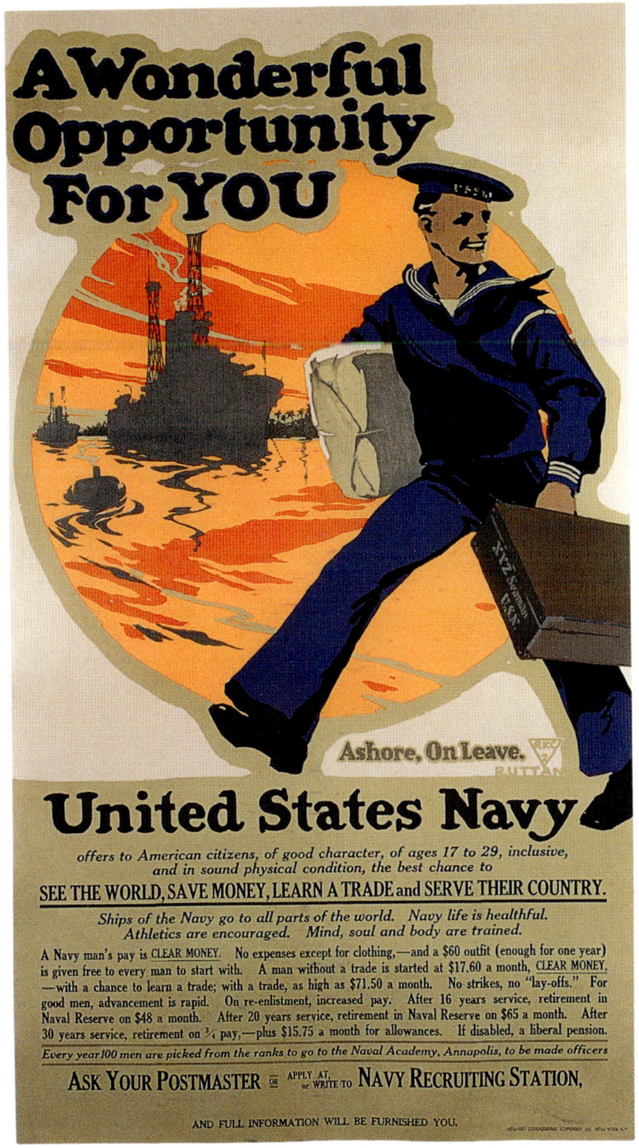

A wonderful opportunity for you, Ruttan, 21" x 38", U. S. Navy, New-Art Lithographic Co., New York. Also exists without bottom text portion. $300-$450.

All together! Enlist in the Navy, Henry Reuterdahl, 31.5" x 43", U. S. Navy, American Litho Co., New York. $400-$550.

Give the world the once over, James H. Doherty, 28" x 43", U. S. Navy, Press Navy Recruiting Bureau, New York. $400-$550. *Courtesy of Swann Galleries.*

U. S. Navy, help your country!, Henry Reuterdahl, 28" x 41", U. S. Navy Latham Litho, Brooklyn, New York. $400-$550.

The U. S. Navy needs men, Raymond Bannister, 28" x 42", U. S. Navy, Louis Roesch, San Francisco. $400-$550. *Courtesy of Swann Galleries.*

Enlist in the Navy, Milton Bancroft, 27" x 41", U. S. Navy, no printer. $400-$550.

Shall this continue?, unsigned, 28" x 42", U. S. Navy, Morgan Litho Co., Cleveland, Ohio. $500-$650. Rare and powerful image. *Courtesy of Swann Galleries.*

He is getting our country's signal, are you?, unsigned, 20" x 30", U. S. Navy, no printer. $400-$550.

Marine Recruiting

U. S. Marines soldiers of the sea, unsigned, 30" x 40", U. S. Marines, no printer. $300-$450. This and following 30" x 40" Marines posters are on heavy glossy stock paper and are printed by halftone process.

U. S. Marines, first to fight for democracy, L. A. Shafer, 30" x 40", U. S. Marines, no printer. $500-$650. Scarce poster showing airship.

U. S. Marine, be a sea soldier, Clarence Underwood, 30" x 40", U. S. Marines, no printer. $400-$550.

U. S. Marines soldiers of the sea, Bruce Moore, 30" x 40", U. S. Marines, no printer. $400-$550.

First to fight, Sidney Reisenberg, U. S. Marines, no printer, 1917. $400-$550.

U. S. Marines first to fight in France, unsigned, 30" x 40" U. S. Marines, no printer. $400-$550.

U. S. Marines soldiers of the sea, J. C. Leyendecker, 30" x 40", U. S. Marines, no printer. $400-$550.

Spirit of 1917, unsigned, 30" x 40", U. S. Marines, no printer. $400-$550.

First in the fight- always faithful- be a U. S. Marine!, James Montgomery Flagg, 27" x 42", U. S. Marines, no printer. $750-$1000. Scarce and popular image.

Be a U. S. Marine!, James Montgomery Flagg, 27.5" x 39.5", U. S. Marines, no printer. $750-$1000.

Travel? Adventure? Answer-join the Marines!, James Montgomery Flagg, 30" x 40", U. S. Marines, no printer. $2500-$3500. Very rarely found, and very desirable. *Courtesy of Swann Galleries.*

Tell that to the Marines!, James Montgomery Flagg, 29" x 40", U. S. Marines, no printer. $400-$550.

U. S. Marines, soldiers of the sea, Bruce Moore, 18" x 26", U. S. Marines, no printer. $200-$300.

Untitled, unsigned, 18" x 26", U. S. Marines, no printer. $200-$300. Issued with metal strips top and bottom.

Untitled, Sidney Reisenberg, 18" x 26", U. S. Marines, no printer. $200-$300. Issued with metal strips top and bottom.

The U. S. Marines want you, unsigned, 21" x 28", U. S. Marines, no printer. $400-$550. Reminiscent of James Montgomery Flagg's Uncle Sam image, but by unknown artist.

This device on hat or helmet means U. S. Marines, C. B. Falls, 28" x 41", U. S. Marines, no printer. $300-$450. Relatively common. Scarcer variant exists with small portraits in upper corners.

U. S. Marines, active service on land and sea, Sidney Reisenberg, 28" x 42", U. S. Marines, no printer. $500-$650. Scarce and colorful.

E-e-e-yah-yip, C. B. Falls, 21" x 28", U. S. Marines, no printer. $200-$300.

If you want to fight! Join the Marines, Howard Chandler Christy, 30" x 40", U. S. Marines, no printer. $1750-$2500. Christy's only Marine recruiting poster, scarce and popular.

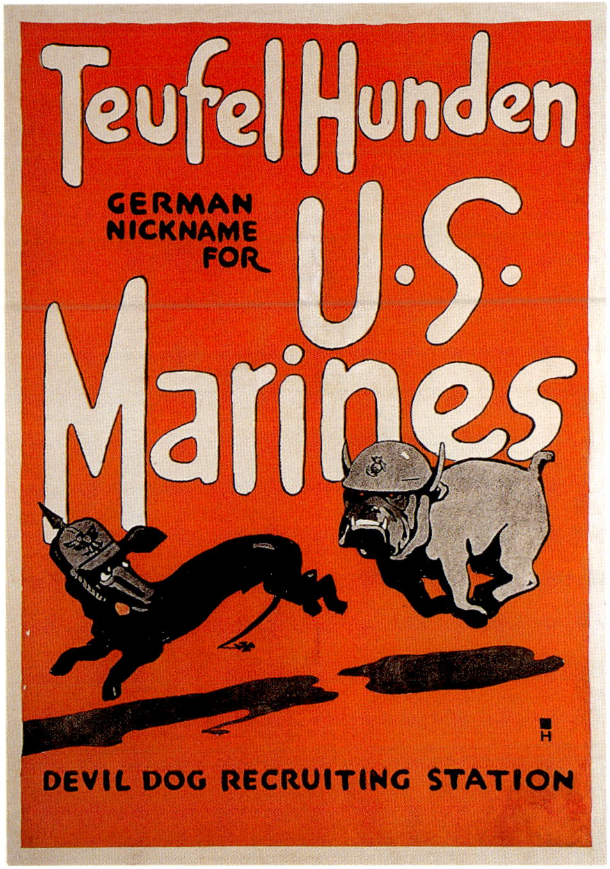

Teufel Hunden, German nickname for U. S. Marines, signed H., 19" x 28", U. S. Marines, no printer. $400-$550.

He did his duty, signed P. W., 21" x 27", U. S. Marines, no printer. $200-$300.

Another notch Chateau Thierry, Adolf Triedler, 30" x 40", U. S. Marines, no printer. $400-$550.

Air Service Recruiting

Join the Army Air Service be an American eagle!, Charles Livingston Bull, 20.5" x 27", Army Air Service, Alpha Litho Co., New York. $2000-$3000. Very scarce and popular.

Join the Air Service and serve in France, J Paul Verrees, 25" x 37", Army Air Service, Ketterlinus, Philadelphia. $1500-$2000. Fine and very scarce. *Courtesy of Swann Galleries.*

For action enlist in the Air Service, Otho Cushing, 19" x 25", Army Air Service, no printer. $900-$1200. *Courtesy of Swann Galleries.*

Our Navy's Aviation Corps, Harold Von Schmidt, 27.5" x 41.5", U. S. Navy, Galloway Litho, San Francisco. $1200-$1500. *Courtesy of Swann Galleries.*

Aviation, Fly with the U. S. Marines, Howard Chandler Christy, 30" x 40", U. S. Marines, no printer. $1750-$2500. *Courtesy of Swann Galleries.*

Other Services Recruiting

Your country calls, Lloyd Myers, 21.5" x 28", Albert Frank and Co., Hamilton Press. $300-$450.

Help win the war with your brain & brawn, Edward Buyer, 25.5" x 38", Ordnance Department, U. S. A, Burleigh Litho Co., Troy, New York. $500-$650. Rarely seen and unusual.

Britishers you're needed, Lloyd Myers, 28" x 41", British and Canadian Recruiting Mission, Albert Frank and Sons. $400-$550.

Enlist, on which side of the window are you?, Laura Brey, 25.5" x 39", U. S. Army, National Printing and Engraving Co., Chicago. $750-$1000. Scarce. *Courtesy of Swann Galleries.*

Treat 'em rough! Join the Tanks, Angiet Hutaf, 14" x 19.25", United States Tank Corps, National Printing and Engraving Co., Chicago, $600-$750. Also comes in larger 28" x 41.5" format, value $2500-$3500. Very scarce and popular, only large tank recruiting poster. *Courtesy of Swann Galleries.*

Know him by this sign, Barton Matteson, 20.25" x 26.5", Medical Corps, U. S. Army, A.G.O. No. 207. $600-$750. Scarce Medical Corps recruiting.

Czechoslovaks! Join our free colors!, Vojtech Preissig, 25" x 36", Wentworth Institute, Boston. $400-$550. One of a large series of scarce posters printed by Wentworth Institute, mostly pertaining to Czechoslovakia. *Courtesy of Swann Galleries.*

You drive a car here- why not a transport in France?, H. Blyleven Esselen, 19" x 27.5", American Field Service, no printer. $200-$300. Unusual poster printed on grey watermarked paper, a small hoard of these posters was found in France.

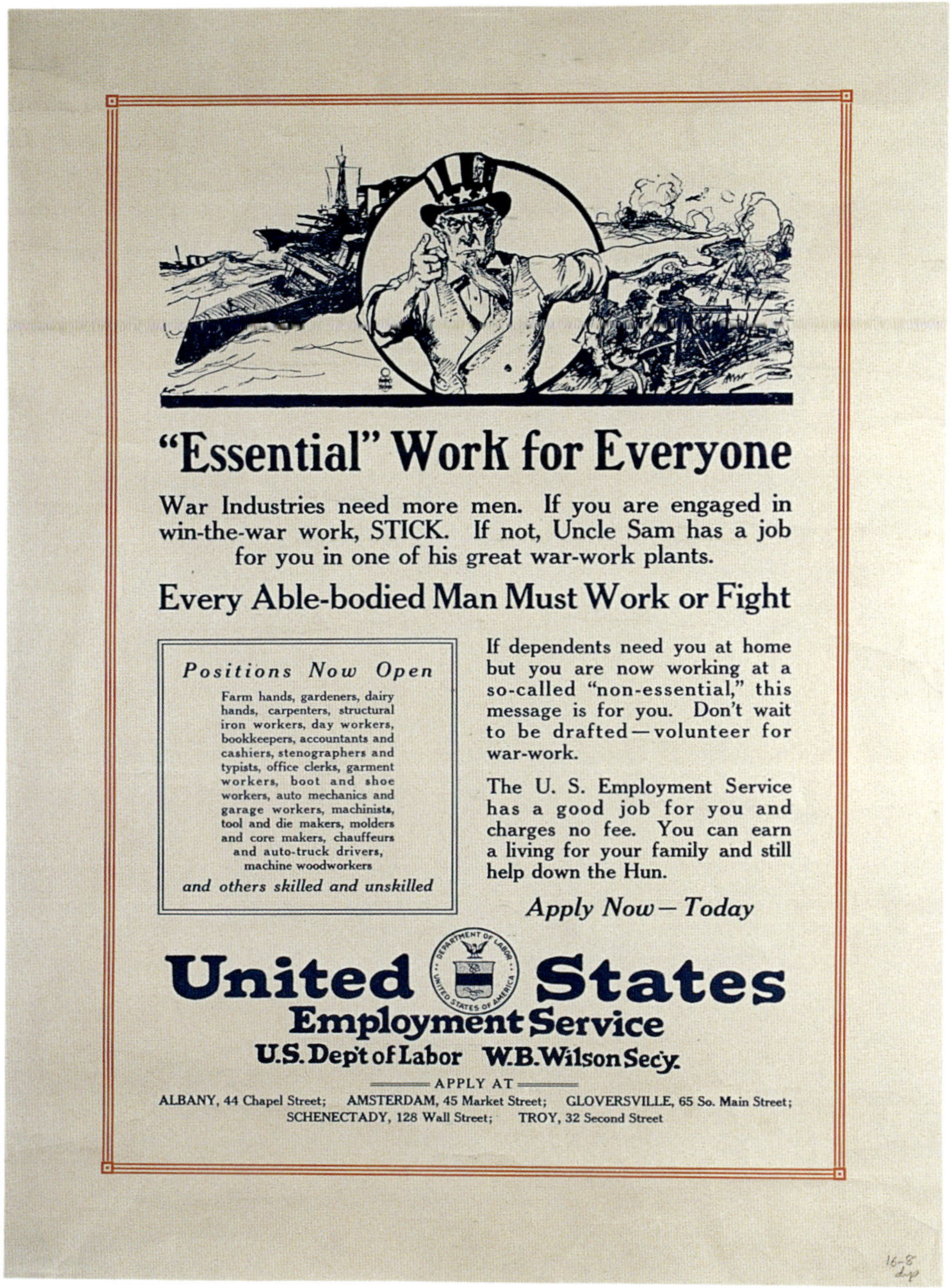

"Essential" work for everyone, unsigned, 18" x 25", United States Employment Service, no printer. $100-$150.

Come on, boys!, unsigned, 22" x 28", National Guard, Edward Stern Co., Philadelphia. $200-$300.

Uncle Sam needs leaders of boys, unsigned, 28" x 41", Boy Scouts of America, Sackett and Wilhelms Co., New York. $1500-$2000. Very rare Scoutmaster recruiting poster.

American Field Service, Nuyttens, 22.5" x 34", American Field Service, Merchants Co., Chicago. $300-$450.

The Motor Corps of America, Helene Jones, 30" x 40", The Motor Corps of America, no printer. $750-$1000. *Courtesy of Swann Galleries.*

The Motor Corps of America, Howard Chandler Christy, 33" x 42.5", The Motor Corps of America, no printer. $1500-$2000. *Courtesy of Swann Galleries.*

Yes sir- I am here!, Edward Penfield, 27" x 39.5", The Motor Corps of America, Carey Print Litho, New York. $1500-$2000. Penfield's rarest WWI poster. *Courtesy of Swann Galleries.*

Wanted 25000 student nurses, Milton Bancroft, 26.5" x 40.5", U. S. Student Nurse Reserve, John H. Eggers Co. $300-$450.

Woman your country needs you!, unsigned (possibly Evelyn Rumsey Carey), 30" x 46", State and National Councils of Defense, no printer. $750-$1000. Rarely seen women's service poster. *Courtesy of Swann Galleries.*

Women Awake!, Hazel Roberts, 19" x 25", Navy League, Andrew B. Graham, Washington D.C., $750-$1000. Very scarce women's service poster. *Courtesy of Swann Galleries.*

War clouds gather!, Hazel Roberts, 19" x 25", Navy League, no printer, $750-$1000. Scarce women's service poster. *Courtesy of Swann Galleries.*

United States Shipping Board

The tidal wave, Joseph Clement Coll, 20" x 30", U. S. Shipping Board, Thomsen-Ellis, Baltimore, $400-$550. *Courtesy of Swann Galleries.*

Hip-hip! Another ship-another victory, Wright, 40" x 60", U. S. Shipping Board, Forbes, Boston. $500-$650.

Teamwork builds ships, W. Stevens, 36" x 51", U. S. Shipping Board, Forbes, Boston. $1500-$2500. Scarce and very popular.

Nothing stops these men let nothing stop you, H. Giles, 39.5" x 54", U. S. Shipping Board, John H. Eggers Co., New York. $500-$650.

Your work means victory, Fred J. Hoertz, 28" x 38", U. S. Shipping Board, Ketterlinus, Philadelphia. $300-$450.

Together we win, James Montgomery Flagg, 30" x 40", U. S. Shipping Board, W. F. Powers Co., New York. $600-$750.

Teamwork wins, Hibbard Kline, 26.5" x 41", U. S. Shipping Board, Thomsen-Ellis Co., Baltimore and New York. $400-$550.

I shall expect every man who is not a slacker, Herbert Paus, 29" x 43", U. S. Navy, H. C. Miner Co., New York. $300-$450. Uncommon production incentive poster.

Rivets are bayonets drive them home!, Sheridan, 25" x 38", U. S. Shipping Board, Thomsen Ellis Co., Baltimore. $400-$550.

On the job for victory, Jonas Lie, 30" x 40", U. S. Shipping Board, W. F. Powers Co., New York. $600-$750. Also seen in 38" x 56" format, value $1500-$2000.

Make every minute count for Pershing, Adolph Triedler, 21" x 26", U. S. Shipping Board, no printer. $300-$450.

Team work wins, Roy Hull Still, 27" x 39", Ordnance Department U. S. Army, John H. Eggers Co., New York. $600-$750. Scarce Army work incentive poster. *Courtesy of Robert Segel.*

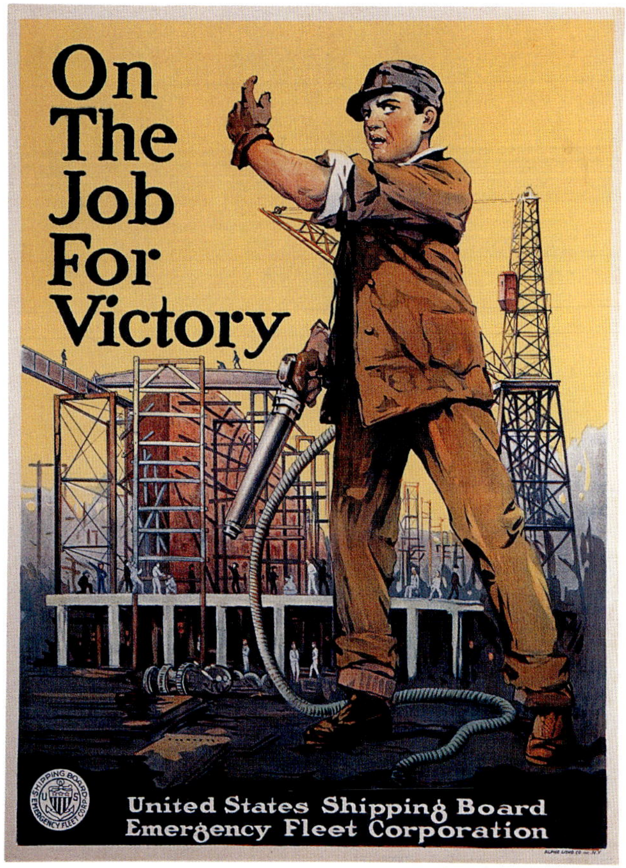

On the job for victory, unsigned, 20.5" x 28", U. S. Shipping Board, Alpha Litho Co., New York. $300-$450.

United States Food Administration

Food will win the war, Sidney Reisenberg, 20" x 30", U. S. Food Administration, Rusling Wood, New York. $400-$550.

Italian Variant (Food will win the war), Sidney Reisenberg, 20" x 30", U. S. Food Administration, Rusling Wood, New York. $600-$750. *Courtesy of Swann Galleries.*

Yiddish Variant (Food will win the war), Sidney Reisenberg, 20" x 30", U. S. Food Administration, Rusling Wood, New York. $1500-$2000. *Courtesy of Swann Galleries.*

Hunger breeds madness, Emil Grebs, 20" x 30", U. S. Food Administration, Schmidt Litho, San Francisco. $300-$400. Scarce. *Courtesy of Swann Galleries.*

They are giving all, will you send them wheat?, Harvey Dunn, 35.5" x 55.5", U. S. Food Administration, W. F. Powers Co., New York. $500-$650. Uncommon larger format conservation poster.

Don't let up, F. Luis Mora, 14" x 21", U. S. Food Administration, Wynkoop Hallenbeck Crawford Co. $150-$200.

Save the products of the land, Charles Livingston Bull, 20" x 30", U. S. Food Administration, Heywood Strasser and Voigt Litho Co., New York. $600-$750. Very scarce and beautiful poster, in much demand.

Food don't waste it, unsigned, 21" x 29", U. S. Food Administration, W. F. Powers Co., New York. $50-$75.

Official pictures of the United States Food Administration, Illion, 29.5" x 45", U. S. Food Administration, W. F. Powers Co. Litho, New York. $200-$300.

Hunger, Raleigh, 21" x 29", U. S. Food Administration, no printer. $100-$150.

Will you help the women of France?, Edward Penfield, 37" x 56", U. S. Food Administration, W. F. Powers Co., New York. $1200-$1500. *Courtesy of Swann Galleries.*

Don't stop saving food, unsigned, 14" x 21.5", U. S. Food Administration, M. B. Brown, Printing Co., New York. $50-$75.

To serve our country, unsigned, 12" x 19", U. S. Food Administration, no printer. $75-$100.

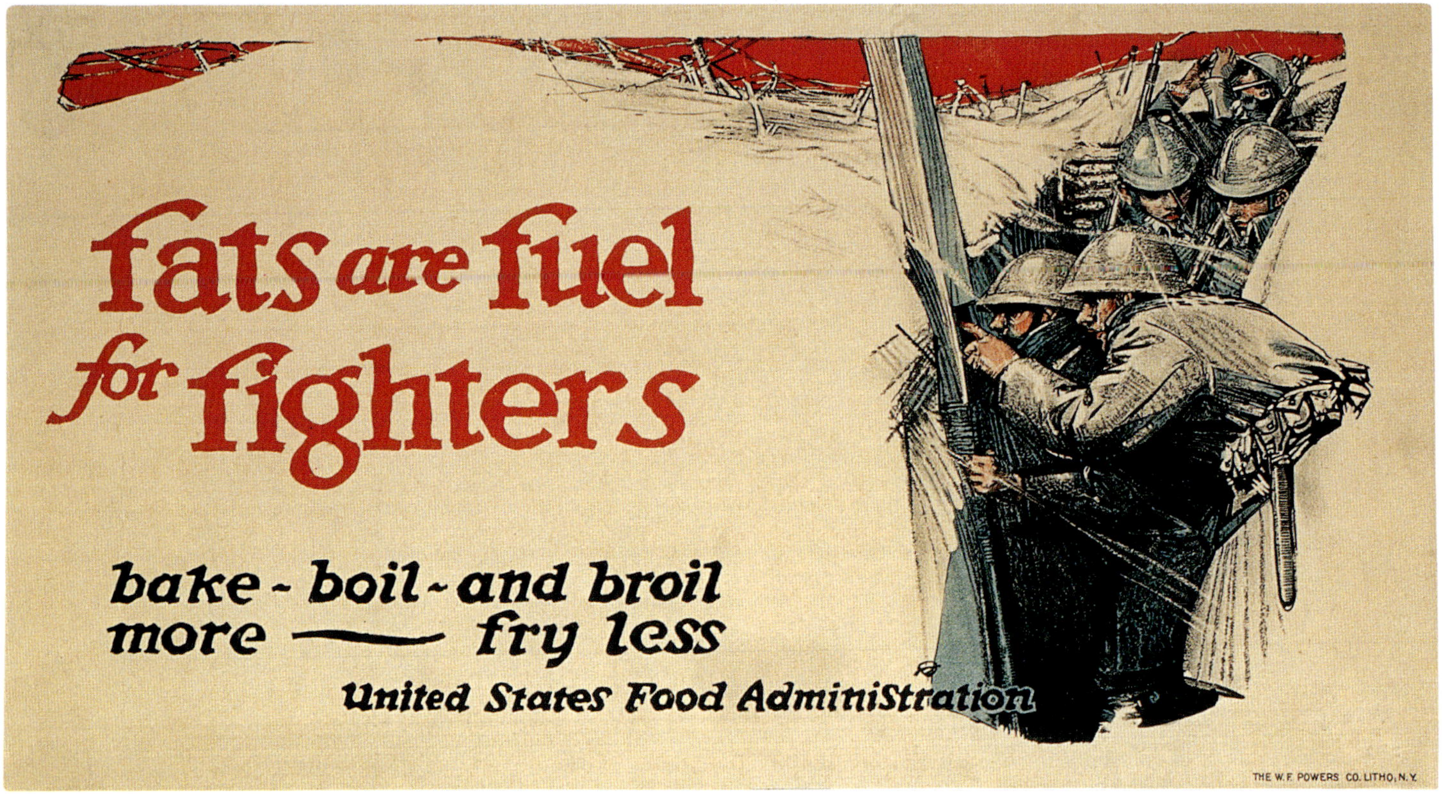

Fats are fuel for fighters, unsigned, 11" x 20.5", U. S. Food Administration, W. F. Powers Co., New York. $100-$150. Bus/trolley poster on card stock.

Save food, unsigned, 10" x 38", U. S. Food Administration, no printer. $50-$75.

Lincoln said, unsigned, 20" x 30", U. S. Food Administration, Edwards and Deutsch Litho Co., Chicago. $100-$150.

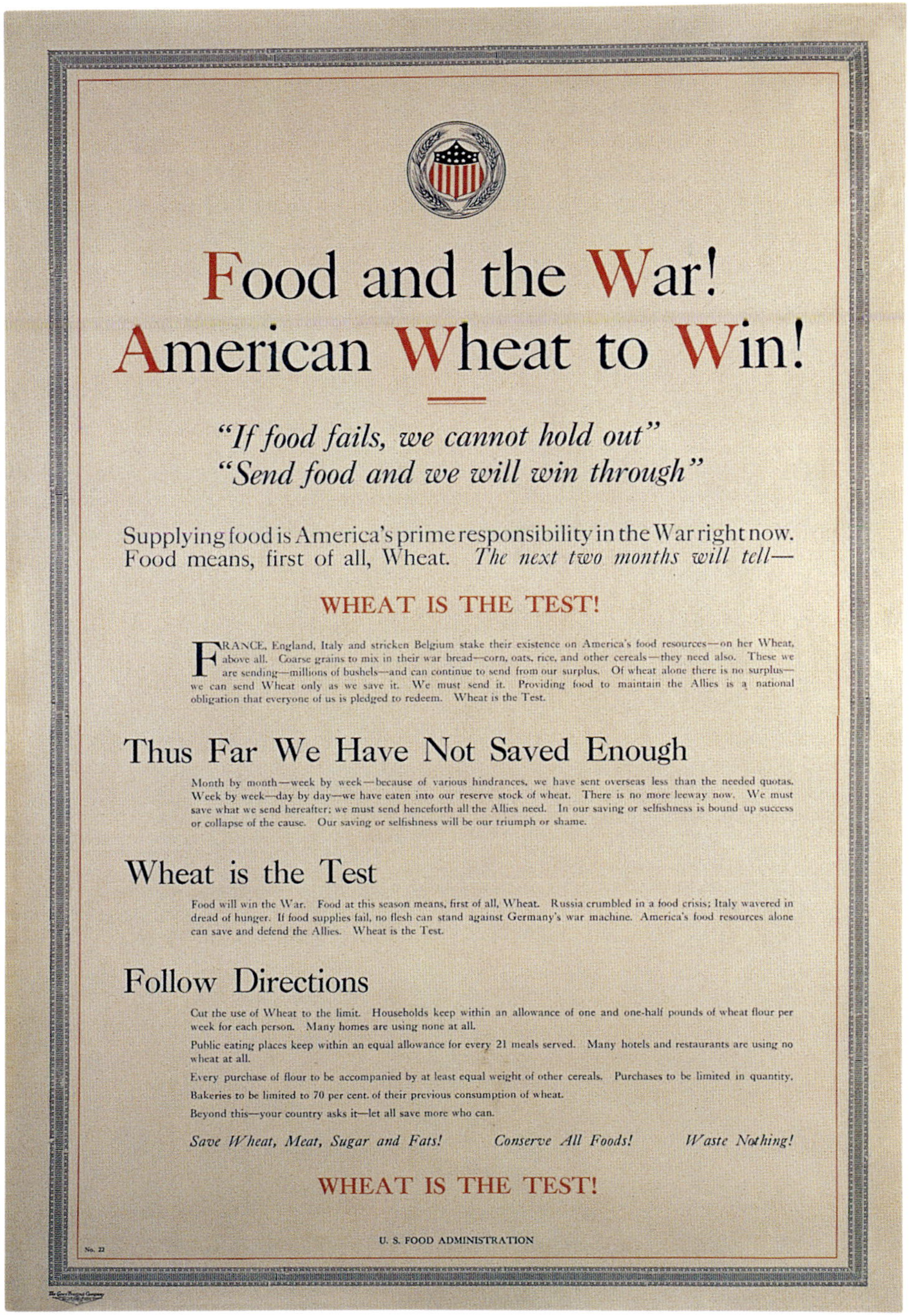

Food and the war!, unsigned, 20" x 29.5", U. S. Food Administration, Carey Printing Co., New York. $75-$100.

This is what God gives us, A. Hendee, 21" x 29", U. S. Food Administration, no printer. $300-$450.

Eat less and let us be thankful, A. Hendee, 21" x 29", U. S. Food Administration, Edwards and Deutsch Litho Co., Chicago. $300-$450.

Don't waste food while others starve!, L. C. Clinker and M. J. Dwyer, 20" x 30", U. S. Food Administration, Heywood Strasser and Voigt Litho Co., New York. $150-$200.

Cardinal Mercier, Illion, 21" x 28", U. S. Food Administration, Latham Litho and Ptg. Co., Brooklyn, New York. $75-$100.

War rages in France, Townsend, 20" x 30", U. S. Food Administration, no printer. $100-$150.

Sir- don't waste while your wife saves, Crawford, 21" x 29", U. S. Food Administration, W. F. Powers Co., New York. $200-$300.

Eat more corn, oats and rye, L. N. Britton, 20" x 30", U. S. Food Administration, Heywood, Strasser and Voigt Litho Co. $400-$550. Reminiscent of German posterist Ludwig Hohlwein. Scarce.

Feed a fighter, W. Morgan, 21" x 29", U. S. Food Administration, no printer. $150-$200.

Wholesome - nutritious foods from corn, Lloyd Harrison, 20" x 30", U. S. Food Administration, Harrison-Landauer Inc., Baltimore. $200-$300.

Keep it coming, Illion, 21" x 29", U. S. Food Administration, W. F. Powers Co. Litho, New York. $150-$200.

The world cry food, William McKee, 20" x 30", U. S. Food Administration, Forbes, Boston. $300-$450.

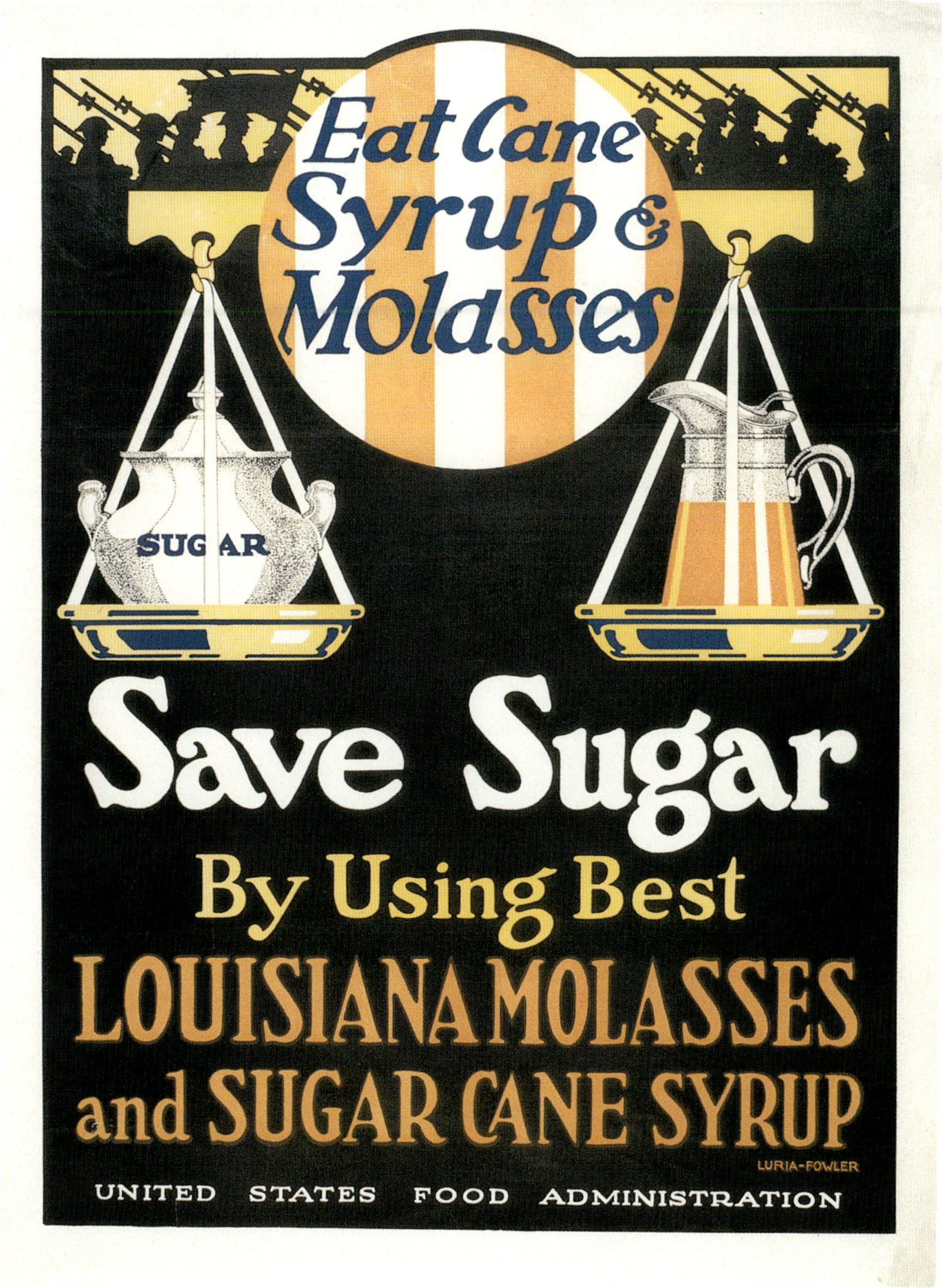

Save sugar, Luria-Fowler, 21" x 28", U. S. Food Administration, Magill-Weinsheimer, Chicago. $200-$300. *Courtesy of Swann Galleries.*

Food is ammunition, J. E. Sheridan, 21" x 28.5", U. S. Food Administration, no printer. $400-$550.

Kosciuszko, Pulawski, Illion, 20.5" x 28.5", U. S. Food Administration, Latham Litho Co. $150-$200.

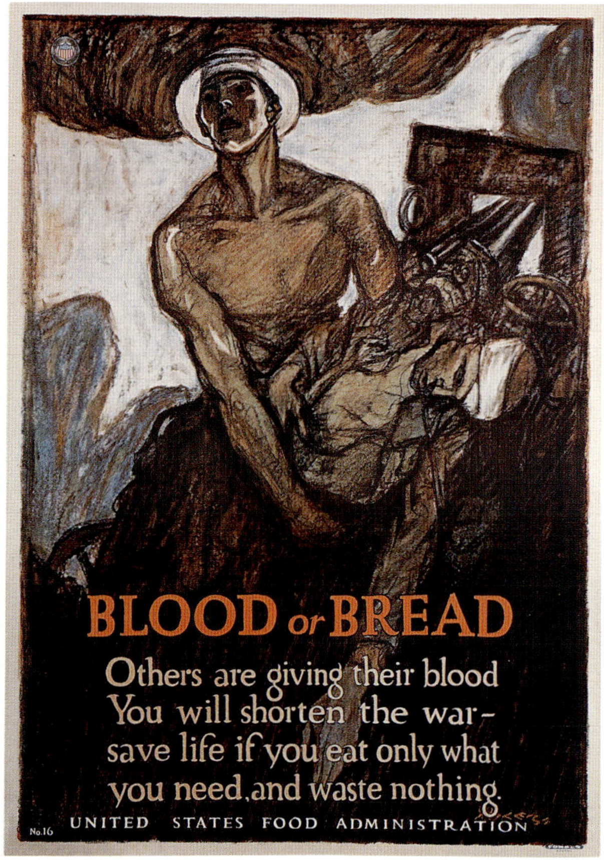

Blood or bread, Raleigh, 21" x 28.5", U. S. Food Administration, Forbes, Boston. $150-$200.

United States Fuel Administration

Jan. 30th Tag your shovel day, unsigned, 12.6" x 19", U. S. Fuel Administration, no printer. $75-$100.

Uncle Sam needs that extra shovelful, F. Sindelar, 20" x 28", U. S. Fuel Administration, Latham Litho and Printing, Brooklyn, New York. $150-$200.

United States Department of Agriculture and Garden Army

Potatoes for patriotism, unsigned, 12" x 18", no printer. $100-$150.

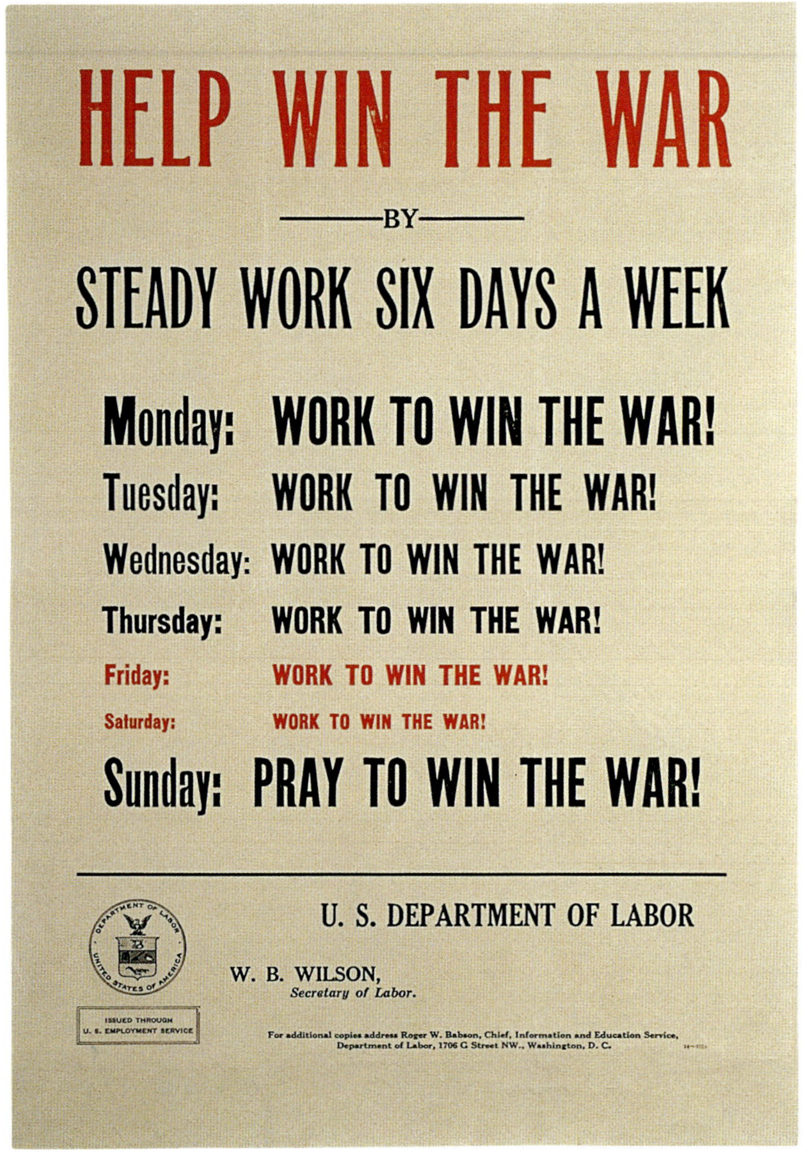

Help win the war, unsigned, 10" x 15", U. S. Department of Labor, no printer. $75-$100.

Your country calls, unsigned, 16" x 22", Iowa Council of National Defense, Gugler Litho Co., Milwaukee. $150-$200. Scarce regional poster.

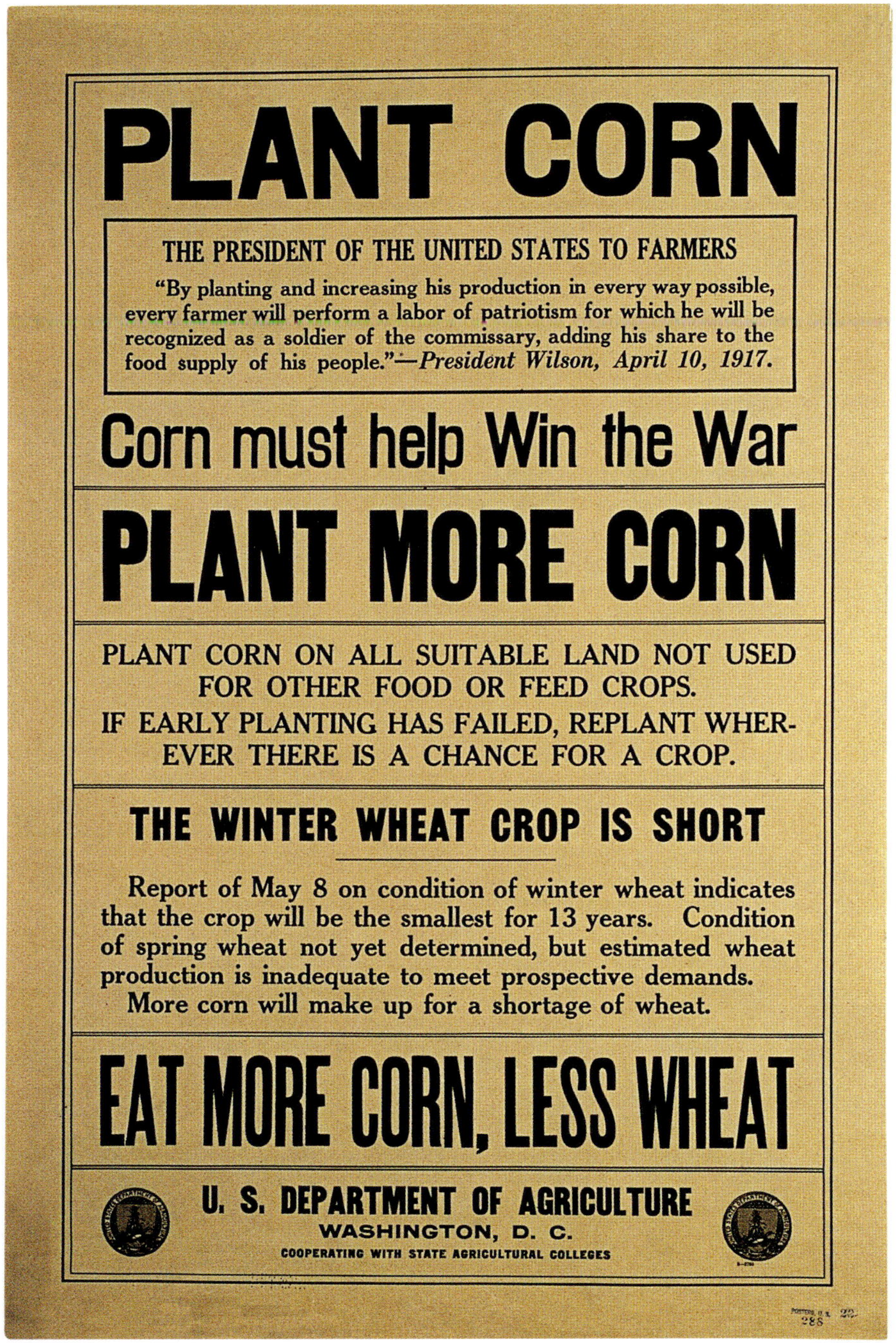

Plant corn, unsigned, 16" x 24", U. S. Department of Agriculture, no printer. $75-$100.

Help feed yourself, unsigned, 16" x 24", U. S. Department of Agriculture, no printer. $100-$150.

Special appeal to farmer patriots, unsigned, 16" x 31.5", U. S. Department of Agriculture, no printer. $100-$150.

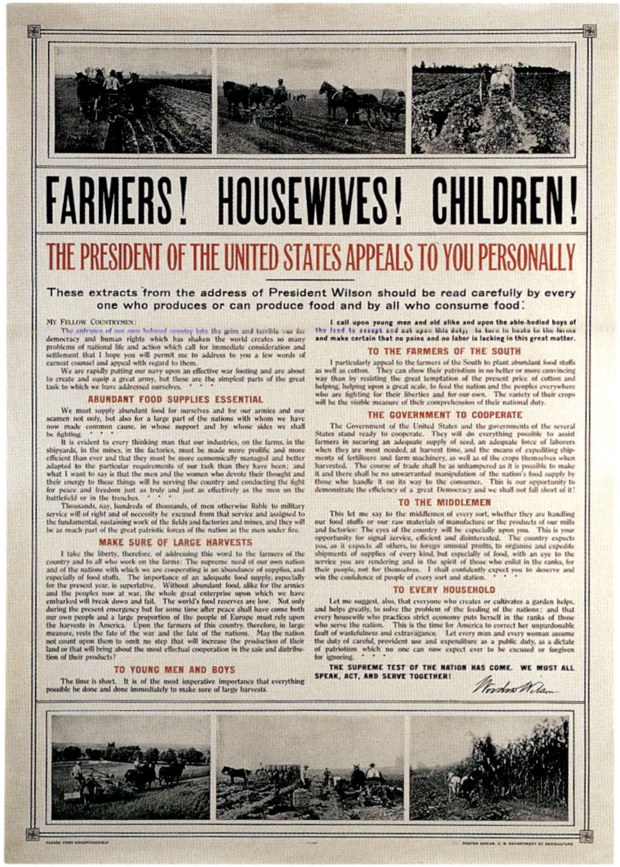

Farmers! Housewives! Children!, unsigned, 21" x 30", U. S. Department of Agriculture, no printer. $100-$150.

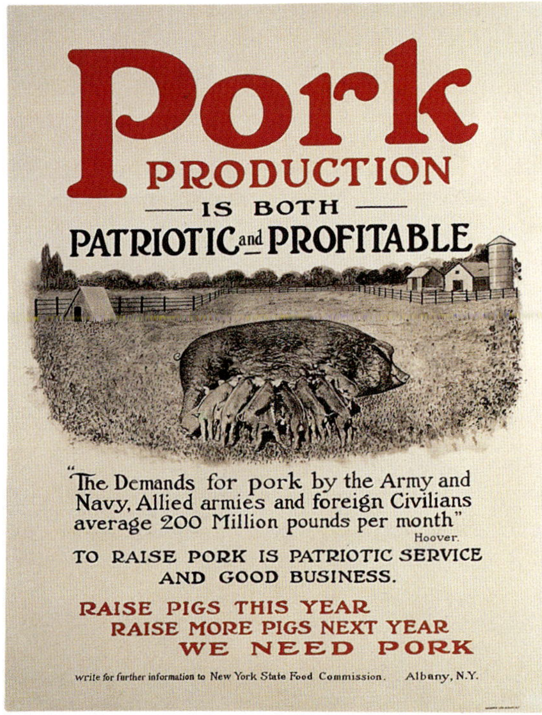

Pork production, unsigned, 18.5" x 24.5", New York State Food Commission, Goodwin Litho, Albany, New York. $200-$300.

Farm for freedom, unsigned, 19" x 24", United States Boy's Working Reserve, no printer. $75-$100.

Stop save peach stones, prune pits, unsigned, 11" x 14", American Red Cross, Gas Defense Division Chemical Warfare Service, no printer. $150-$200. Scarce and unusual.

War gardens over the top, Macinel Wright Enright, 22" x 29", National War Garden Commission. $600-$750. *Courtesy of Swann Galleries.*

War gardens victorious, Macinel Wright Enright, 22" x 29", National War Garden Commission. $600-$750. *Courtesy of Swann Galleries.*

The Woman's Land Army of America, Herbert Paus, 20" x 30", Woman's Land Army. $600-$750. *Courtesy of Swann Galleries.*

Sow the seeds of victory, James Montgomery Flagg, 22" x 33", National War Garden Commission, no printer. $500-$650. Found printed on both paper and cardboard.

Liberty sowing the seeds of victory, Frank DuMond, 22" x 33", National War Garden Commission, no printer. $400-$550. On cardboard stock.

Follow the Pied Piper, Macinel Wright Enright, 16" x 22", United States School Garden Army, The Graphic Co., Washington D.C. $300-$450.

Helping Hoover in our U. S. School Garden, unsigned, 20" x 30", U. S. School Garden Army, no printer. $500-$650.

Raised 'em myself, unsigned, 20" x 30", U. S. School Garden Army, American Lithographic Co., New York. $500-$650.

First Liberty Loan of 1917

The spirit of '17 '76, Ickes, 27" x 41", First Liberty Loan, Ohio Litho Co., Toledo, Ohio. $300-$450. *Courtesy of Swann Galleries.*

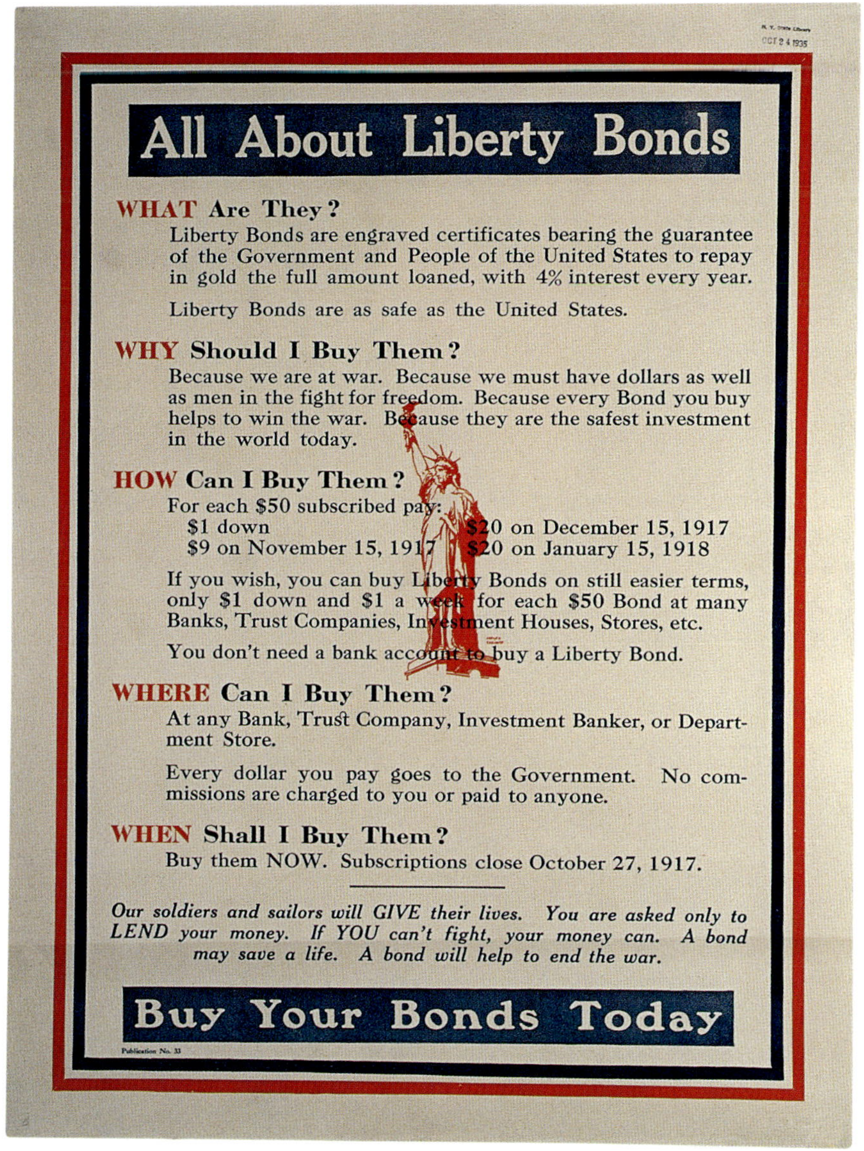

All about Liberty Bonds, unsigned, 18" x 24", First Liberty Loan, no printer. $75-$100.

Uncle Sam is worth $225,000,000,000, unsigned, 14" x 19", First Liberty Loan, no printer. $75-$100.

Have you bought your bond?, Adolph Triedler, 21" x 28", First Liberty Loan, Rusling Wood, New York. $200-$300.

But-the Liberty Bond you buy-it backs them all, James Montgomery Flagg, 18.5" x 24.5", First Liberty Loan, no printer. $200-$300.

You buy a liberty bond lest I perish, C. R. Macauley, 30" x 40", First Liberty Loan, no printer. $300-$450. Also published in 20" x 30" size, value $200-$300.

Let's end it-quick with Liberty Bonds, Maurice Ingres, 28" x 42", First Liberty Loan, Central Litho Co., Cleveland, Ohio. $500-$650.

Buy a Liberty Bond of the U. S. Government, unsigned, 20" x 30", First Liberty Loan, Edwards and Deutsch Litho Co., Chicago. $100-$150.

If you can't enlist, invest!, unsigned, 20" x 29", First Liberty Loan, no printer. $200-$300.

Second Liberty Loan of 1917

The Hun- his mark blot it out, J. Allen St. John, 27.5" x 42.5", Second Liberty Loan, Brett Litho Co., New York. $200-$300. Also published in 20" x 30" size, value $100-$150.

Our daddy is fighting at the front for you, Dewey, 20" x 30", Second Liberty Loan, T. F. Moore, New York. $200-$300.

Women! Help America's sons win the war, R. H. Porteous, 20" x 30", Second Liberty Loan, Edwards and Deutsch Litho, Chicago. $200-$300.

"Ammunition!", Vincent, 20" x 30", Second Liberty Loan, Ketterlinus, Philadelphia. $300-$450.

You buy a liberty bond lest I perish!, unsigned, 20" x 30" Second Liberty Loan, no printer. $200-$300.

Shall we be more tender with our dollars, unsigned, 20" x 30", Second Liberty Loan, Edwards and Deutsch Litho, Chicago. $200-$300.

Before sunset, Eugene De Land, 20" x 30", Second Liberty Loan, Sackett and Wilhelms, New York. $200-$300.

Remember your first thrill of American liberty, 20" x 30", Second Liberty Loan, Sackett and Wilhelms Co., New York. $200-$300.

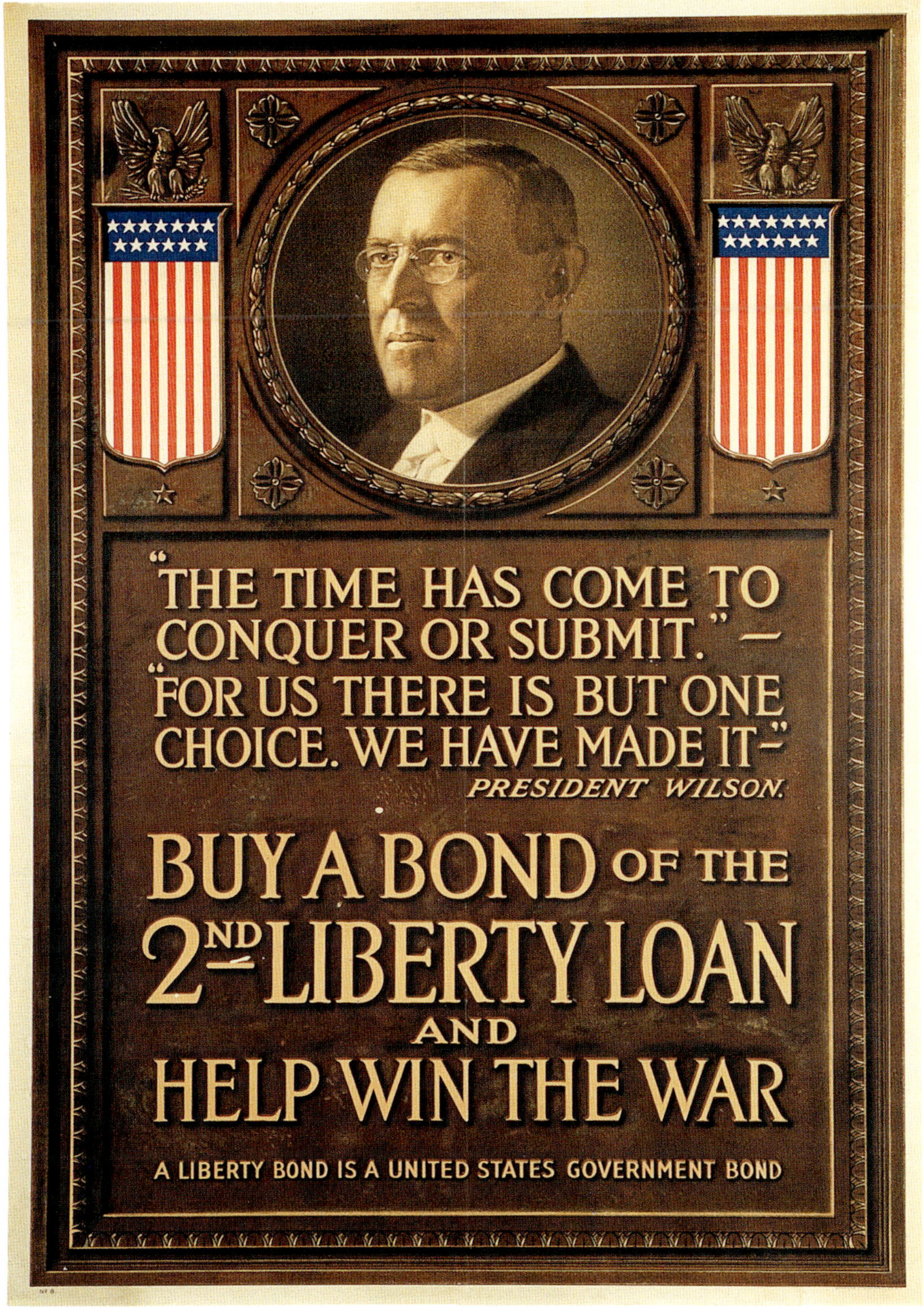

The time has come to conquer or submit, unsigned, 20" x 30", Second Liberty Loan, no printer. $150-$200.

Shall we be more tender with our dollars, Dan Sayre Groesbeck, 20" x 30", Second Liberty Loan, Illinois Litho Co., Chicago. $200-$300.

Owners of Liberty Loan Bonds, unsigned, 11" x 21", Second Liberty Loan, no printer. $75-$100. Trolley poster on cardboard.

Third Liberty Loan

To make the world a decent place to live in, Herbert Paus, 35.5" x 55", Third Liberty Loan, Niagara Litho Co., Buffalo, New York. $400-$550.

After a zeppelin raid in London, Louis Raemaekers, 12" x 19", Third Liberty Loan, Brown Robertson Co. $150-$200.

Lend him a hand, Sarka, 12" x 19", Third Liberty Loan, no printer. $100-$150.

Help win the right to fly this flag, R. C. Boswell, 25" x 38.5", Third Liberty Loan, Capital Pub Inc., Washington, D.C. $100-$150.

Remember! The flag of liberty support it!, unsigned, 20" x 30", Third Liberty Loan, Heywood Strasser and Voigt Litho Co., New York. $200-$300.

Halt the Hun!, Raleigh, 20" x 30", Third Liberty Loan, Edwards and Deutsch, Chicago. $200-$300.

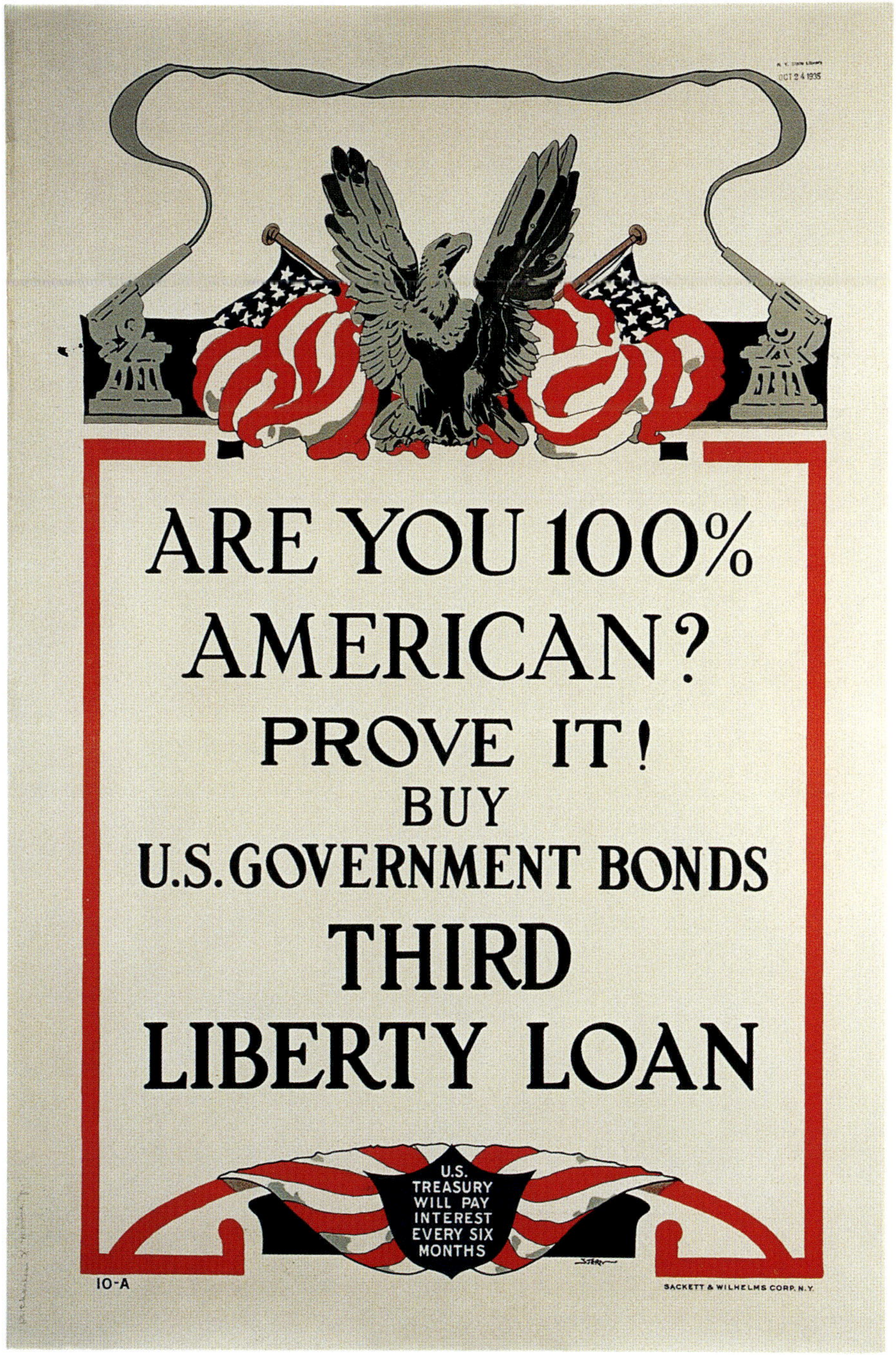

Are you 100% American?, unsigned, 20" x 30", Third Liberty Loan, Sackett and Wilhelms Co., New York. $100-$150.

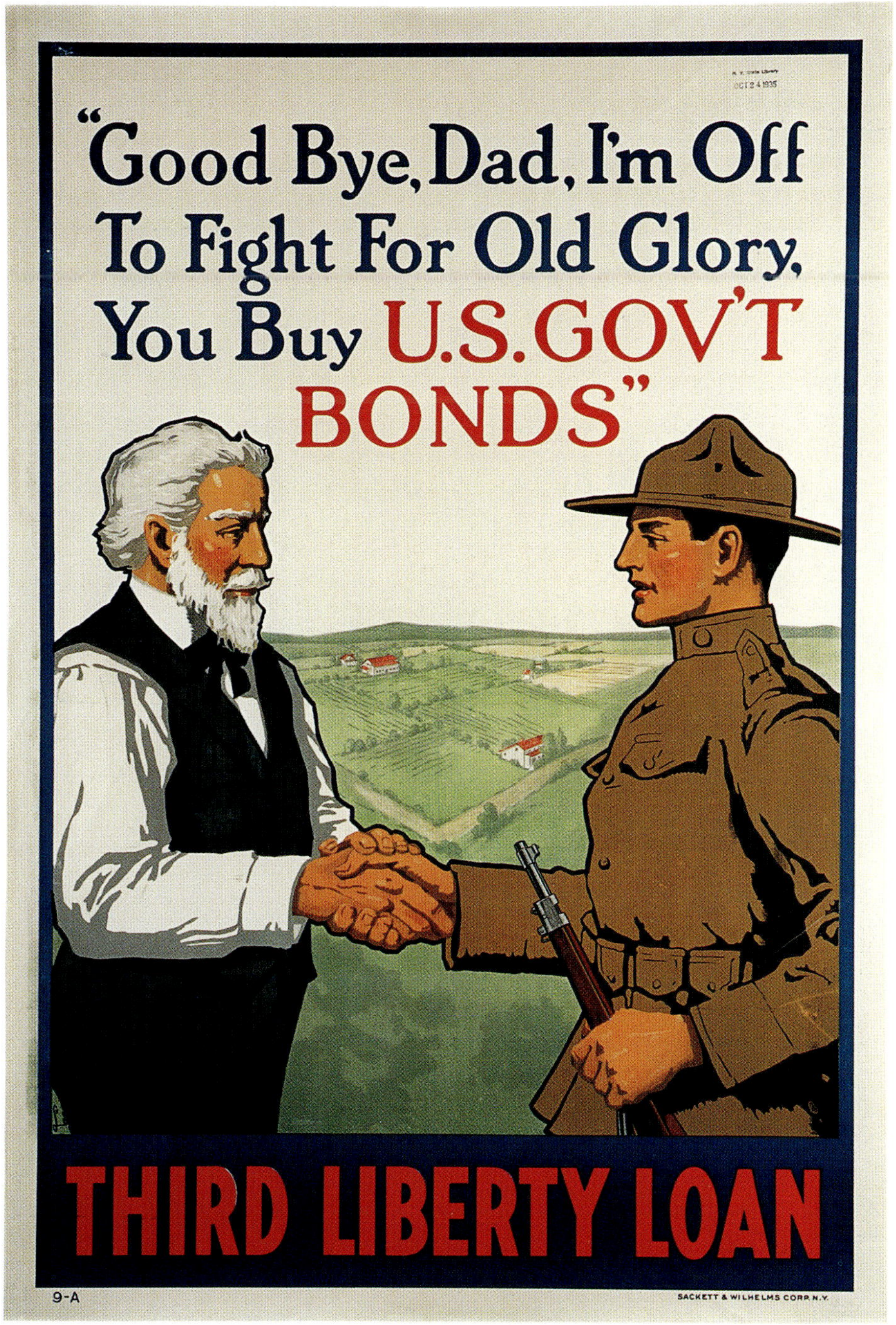

Goodbye dad, unsigned, 20" x 30", Third Liberty Loan, Sackett and Wilhelms, New York. $150-$200.

Buy Liberty Bonds, unsigned, 20" x 30", Third Liberty Loan, American Litho Co., New York. $100-$150.

Ring it again, unsigned, 20" x 30", Third Liberty Loan, Sackett and Wilhelms Co., New York. $100-$150.

My daddy bought me a government bond, unsigned, 20" x 30", Third Liberty Loan, The United States Printing and Litho Co., New York. $150-$200.

Crush the Prussian, unsigned, 27.5" x 41", Third Liberty Loan, no printer. $400-$550.

Keep these off the U. S. A., John Norton, 30" x 40", Third Liberty Loan, Strobridge Litho Co., Cincinnati, Ohio. $400-$550.

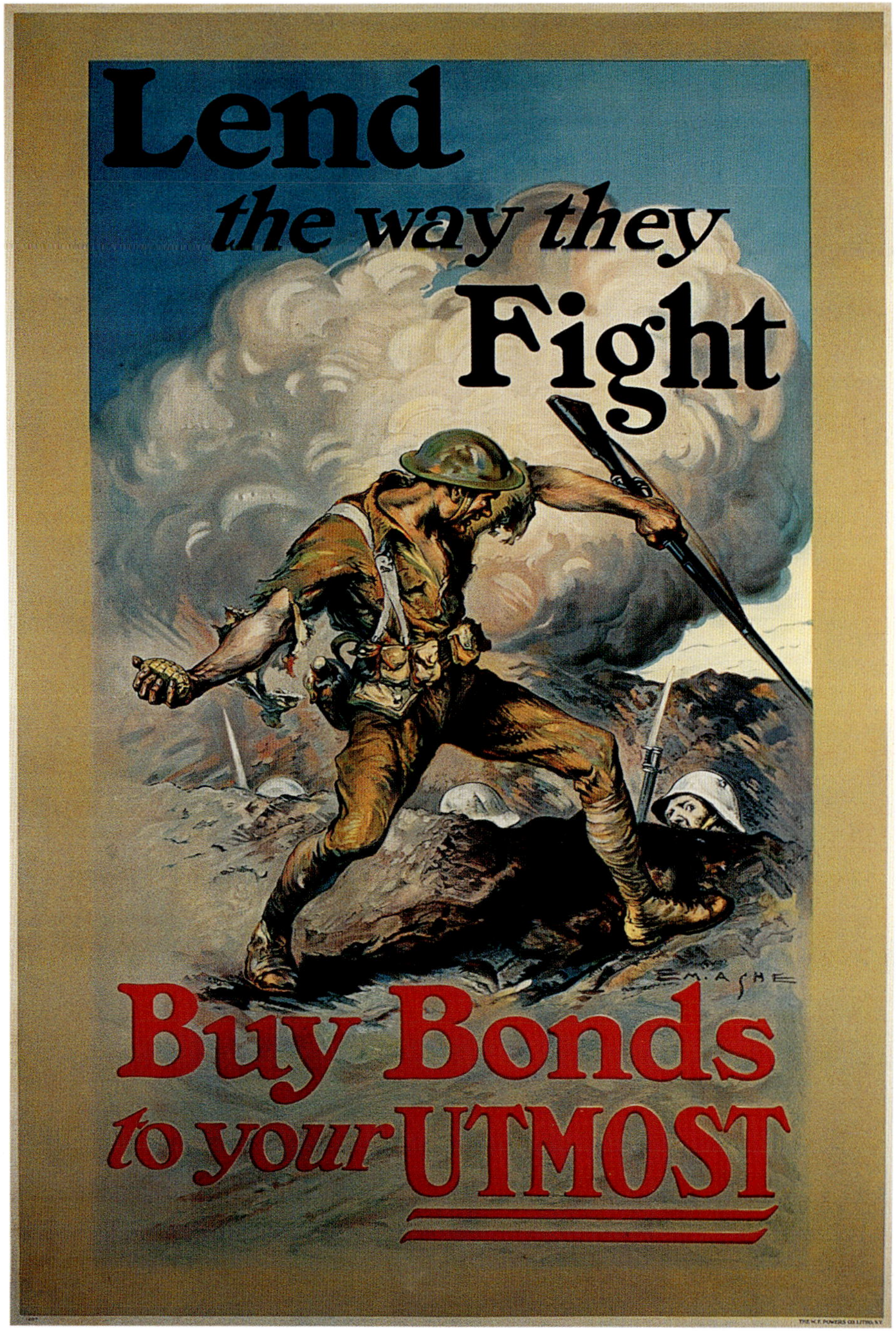

Lend the way they fight, M. Ashe, 27" x 41", Third Liberty Loan, W. F. Powers Co., New York. $300-$450.

Fight or buy bonds, Howard Chandler Christy, 30" x 40", Third Liberty Loan, Forbes, Boston. $400-$550. Also published in 20" x 30", value $300-$400.

U. S. A. Bonds, J. C. Leyendecker, 20" x 30", Boy Scouts of America, American Lithographic Co., New York. $400-$550. Scarce and popular Boy Scout related poster.

Come on! Buy more Liberty Bonds, Walter Whitehead, 20" x 30", Ketterlinus, Philadelphia. $150-$200.

Over the top for you, Sidney Reisenberg, 20" x 30", Third Liberty Loan, Ketterlinus, Philadelphia. $200-$300.

Fourth Liberty Loan

For victory, buy more bonds, J. Scott Williams, 36" x 56", Fourth Liberty Loan, Donaldson Litho Co., Newport, Kentucky. $600-$750. *Courtesy of Swann Galleries.*

To-day buy that Liberty Bond, unsigned, 7" x 11", Fourth Liberty Loan, no printer. $25-$40. This is the handbill size, also seen in 14" x 20" and 20" x 28", value respectively $50-$75 and $75-$100.

Clear-the-way-!!, Howard Chandler Christy, 20" x 30", Fourth Liberty Loan, Forbes, Boston. $300-$400.

Provide the sinews of war, Joseph Pennell, 20" x 21", Fourth Liberty Loan, Heywood Strasser and Voigt, New York. $150-$200. On card stock.

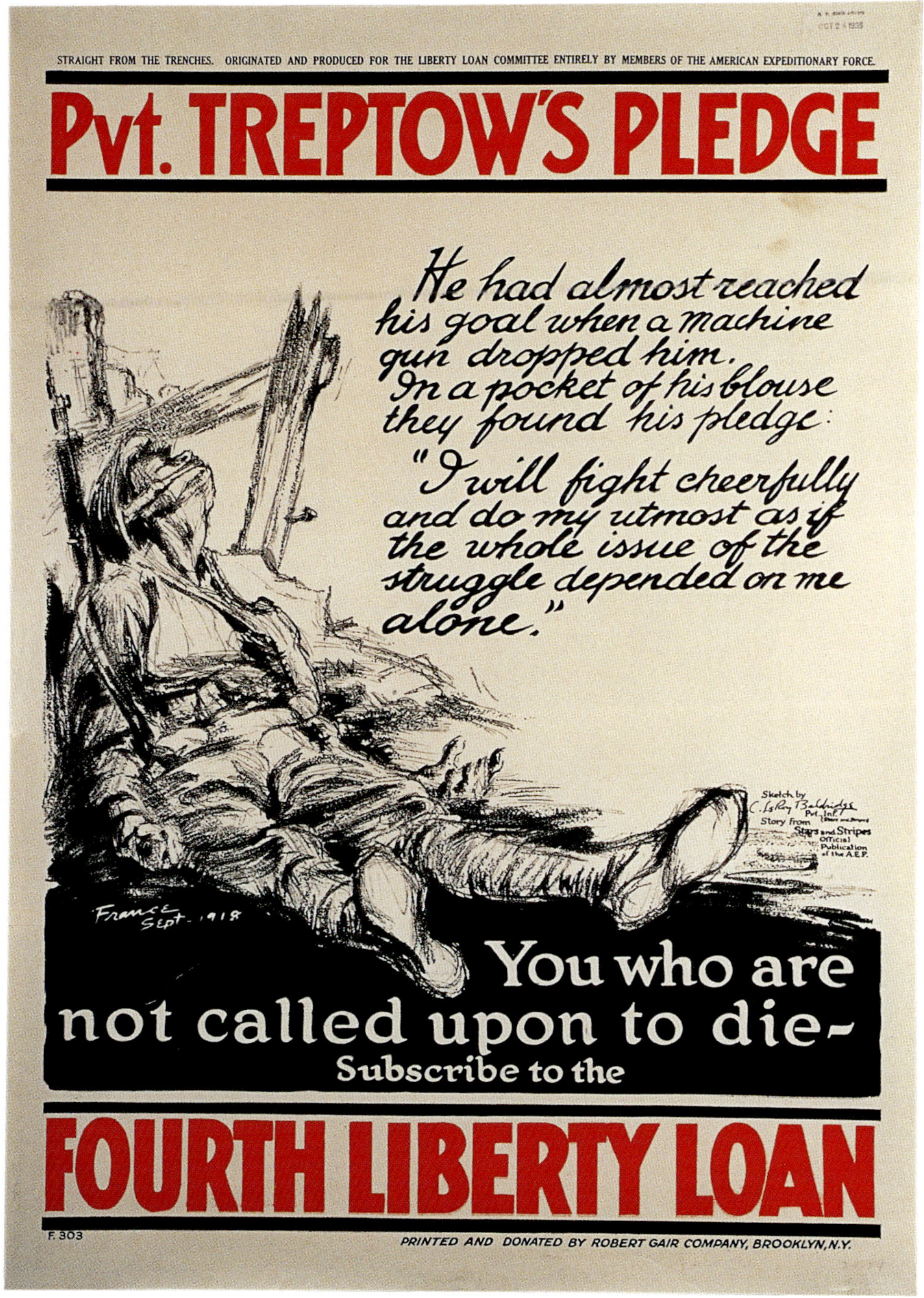

Pvt. Treptow's pledge, C. Leroy Baldridge, 20" x 30", Fourth Liberty Loan, Robert Gair Co., Brooklyn, New York. $100-$150.

Remember Belgium, Ellsworth Young, 20" x 30", Fourth Liberty Loan, United States Printing and Litho Co., New York. $150-$200.

We clear the way, Scott Ethridge, 21" x 28", Fourth Liberty Loan, no printer. $200-$300.

Buy to-day at any bank, S. L. Bush, 22" x 28", Fourth Liberty Loan, no printer. $100-$150. Also seen in two smaller sizes.

That liberty shall not perish from the earth. Joseph Pennell, 30" x 40", Fourth Liberty Loan, Heywood Strasser and Voigt Litho Co., New York. $400-$550. Generally seen on low quality brown paper usually in poor condition, white paper version scarcer and more valuable.

That liberty shall not perish from the earth, Joseph Pennell, 21.5" x 30", Fourth Liberty Loan, Auto Gravure Co., New York. $300-$400. Note slight differences compared to larger format.

Hun or home?, Raleigh, 20" x 30", Fourth Liberty Loan, Edwards and Deutsch, Chicago. $150-$200.

Beat back the Hun with Liberty Bonds, F. Strothmann, 20" x 30", Fourth Liberty Loan, no printer. $200-$300.

The men of the A. E. F. expect that the Fourth Liberty Loan shall be subscribed, unsigned, 22" x 28", Fourth Liberty Loan, no printer. $100-$150. Part of a large series (four illustrated here).

And they struck off a medal for this, unsigned, 22" x 28", Fourth Liberty Loan, no printer. $150-$200. Refers to sinking of the Lusitania and famous German medal commemorating it.

Making dollars into munitions, Edward Annison, 22" x 28", Fourth Liberty Loan, no printer. $100-$150.

Must children die and mothers plead in vain?, Henry P. Raleigh, 30" x 40", Fourth Liberty Loan, no printer. $300-$450.

This is Prussianism!, unsigned, 22" x 28", Fourth Liberty Loan, no printer. $100-$150.

Victory Liberty Loan

Buy Early, unsigned, 20" x 27", Victory Liberty Loan, no printer. $75-$100.

The Victory Loan Flyers, K. Watkins, 20" x 30", Victory Liberty Loan, Sackett and Wilhelms, New York. $300-$450. *Courtesy of Swann Galleries.*

Honor button, unsigned, 10" x 14", Victory Liberty Loan, Heywood Strasser. $50-$75.

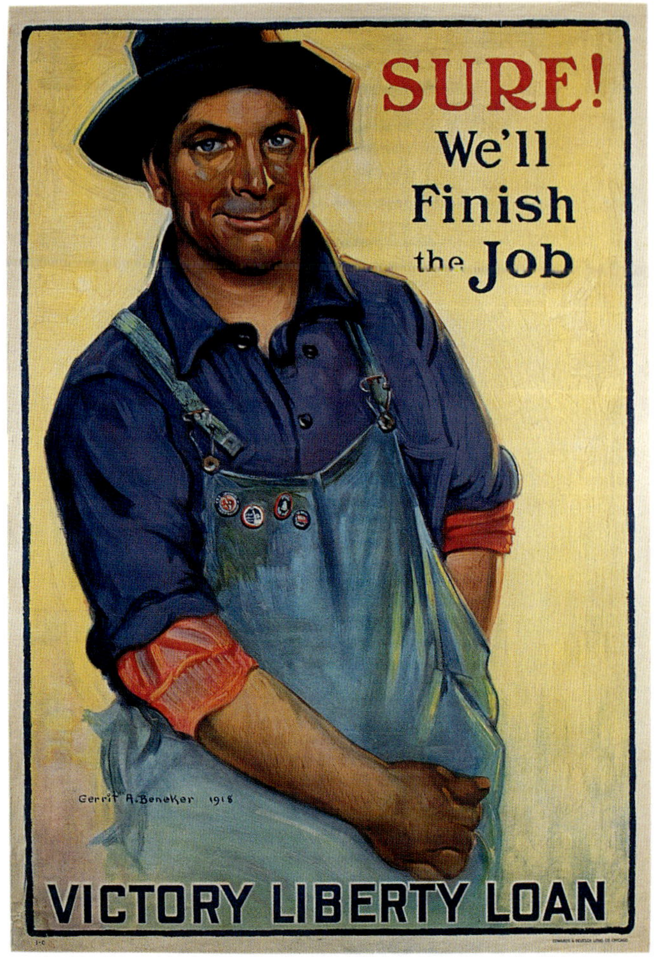

Sure! We'll finish the job, Gerrit A. Beneker, 26" x 38", Victory Liberty Loan, Edwards and Deutsch Litho Co., Chicago. $150-$200. Relatively common.

Finish the job, unsigned, 14" x 21", Victory Liberty Loan, no printer. $50-$75. Also seen in 20" x 30" format, value $75-$100.

V Invest, unsigned, 21" x 56", Victory Liberty Loan, U. S. Printing and Lithograph Co., New York. $300-$450. Scarce.

Show your button, unsigned, 20" x 27", Victory Liberty Loan, no printer. $75-$100

(Hungarian) *On dolgozik*, unsigned, 21" x 28", Victory Liberty Loan, National Printing and Eng. Co., New York. $75-$100. Scarce.

And they thought we couldn't fight, Clyde Forsythe, 20" x 30", Victory Liberty Loan, Ketterlinus, Philadelphia. $100-$150. Also issued in 30" x 40" size, value $200-$300. Relatively common.

Invest, unsigned, 24" x 24", Victory Liberty Loan, no printer. $100-$150. Unusual minimalist, modernist design.

For home and country, Alfred Everett Orr, 20" x 30", Victory Liberty Loan, American Litho Co., New York. $100-$150. Also issued in 30" x 40", value $200-$300. Common.

Invest in the Victory Liberty Loan, L. A. Shafer, 29" x 39", Victory Liberty Loan, W. F. Powers Co., New York. $500-$650.

Americans all!, Howard Chandler Christy, 27" x 40", Victory Liberty Loan, Forbes, Boston. $300-$450.

The most popular button in America, 21" x 28", Victory Liberty Loan, Button Merchants Association of America, Binger, New York. $300-$450. Scarce.

Miscellaneous and Private Loan Posters

If you can't enlist-invest, Windsor McCay, 28" x 42", New York American, Star Co., New York, $600-$750. Also seen in very large and rare three-sheet version, value $900-$1200. *Courtesy of Swann Galleries.*

We own a U. S. Government Bond, Adolph Triedler, 10" x 11.5", no printer. $50-$75. Card stock.

Bonds-which?, Cesare, 14" x 22", New York Evening Post, no printer. $150-$200.

She does not ask for contributions, Frances Adams Halstead, 14" x 21", U. S. Government Bonds, no printer. $100-$150. Scarce smaller variant of U. S. Army recruiting poster *Columbia calls*.

Invest your money with Uncle Sam!, unsigned, 21" x 40", United Cigar Stores Co., no printer. $300-$450. Privately printed, part of larger series on thin paper stock.

Invest your money with Uncle Sam!, signed unclear monogram, 26" x 40", United Cigar Stores Co., no printer. $300-$450. Privately printed, part of larger series on thin paper stock.

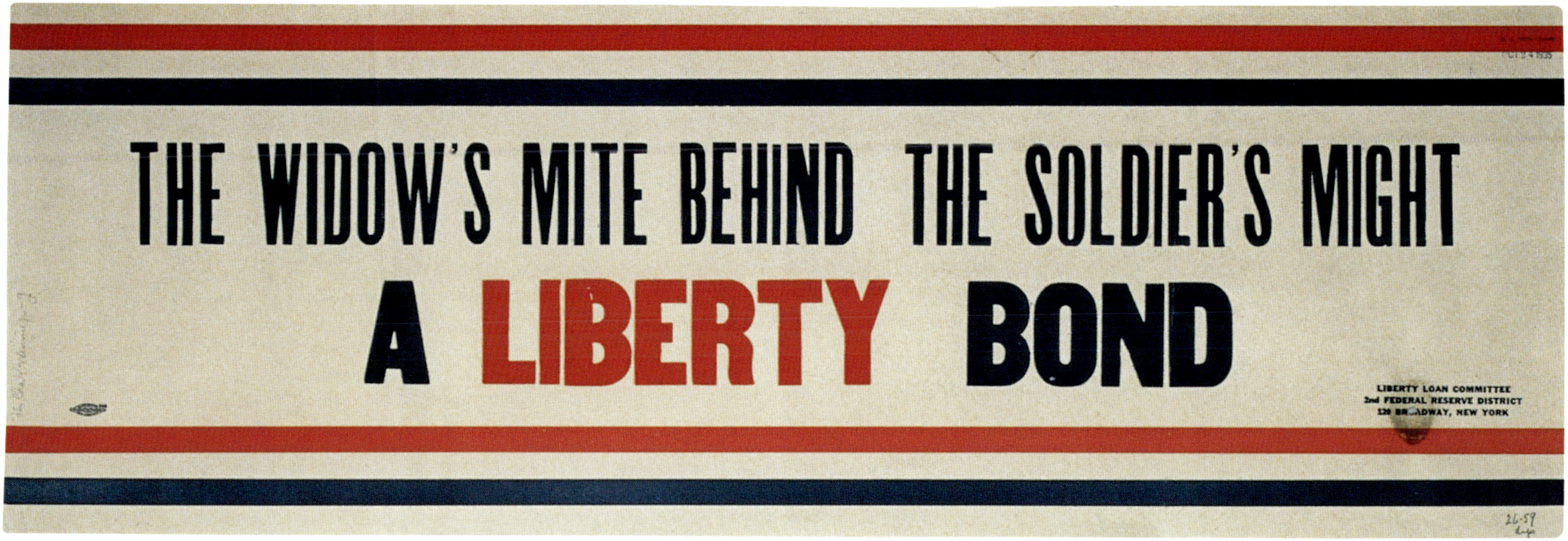

Above: *The widow's mite behind the soldier's might*, unsigned, 10" x 30", no printer. $50-$75.
Below: *Pro-Prussian or Pro-Pershing*, unsigned, 10" x 30", no printer. $50-$75.

A good part of the proceeds of this farm, unsigned, 13" x 28", no printer. $50-$75.

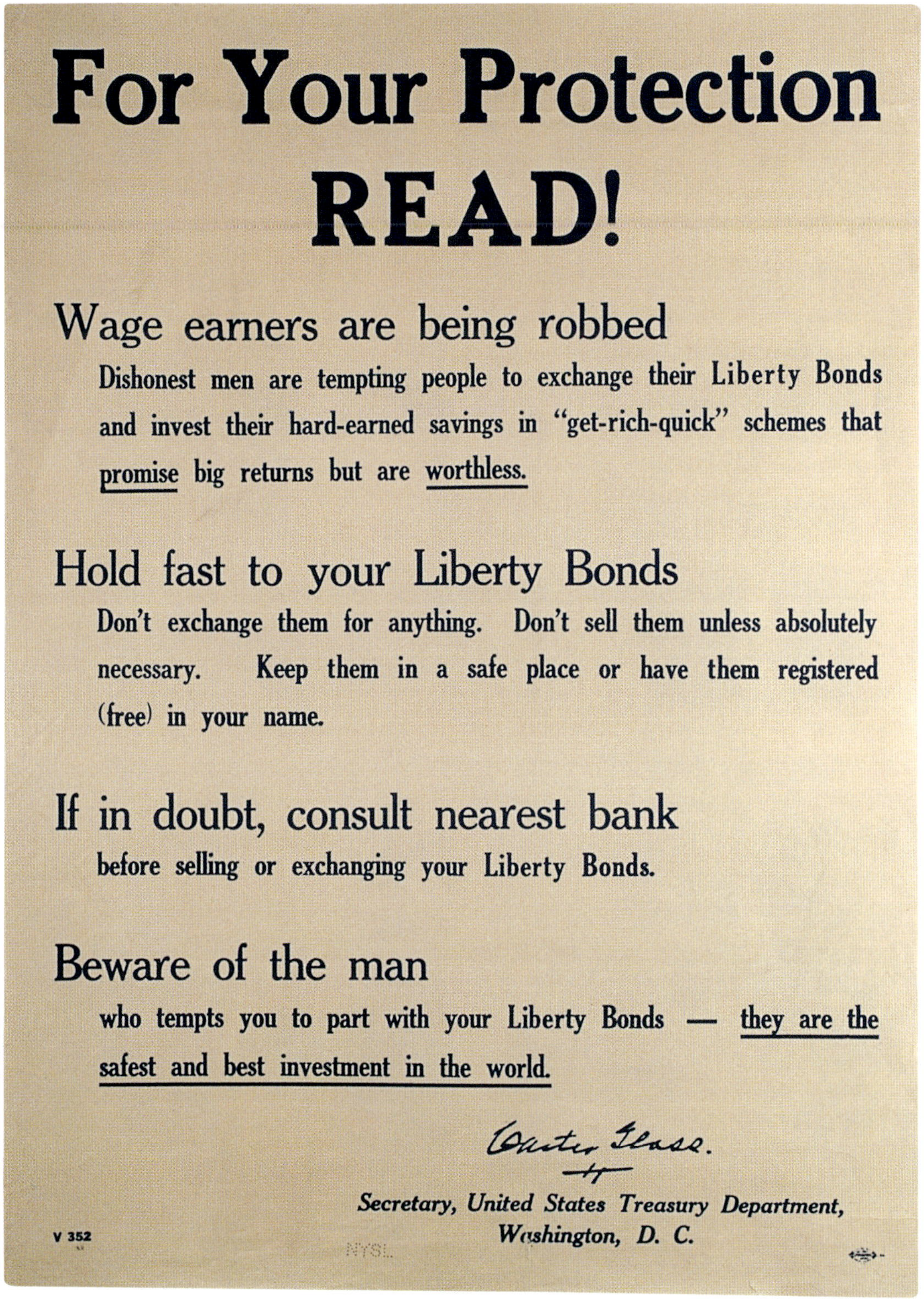

For your protection Read!, unsigned, 20" x 28", no printer. $50-$75.

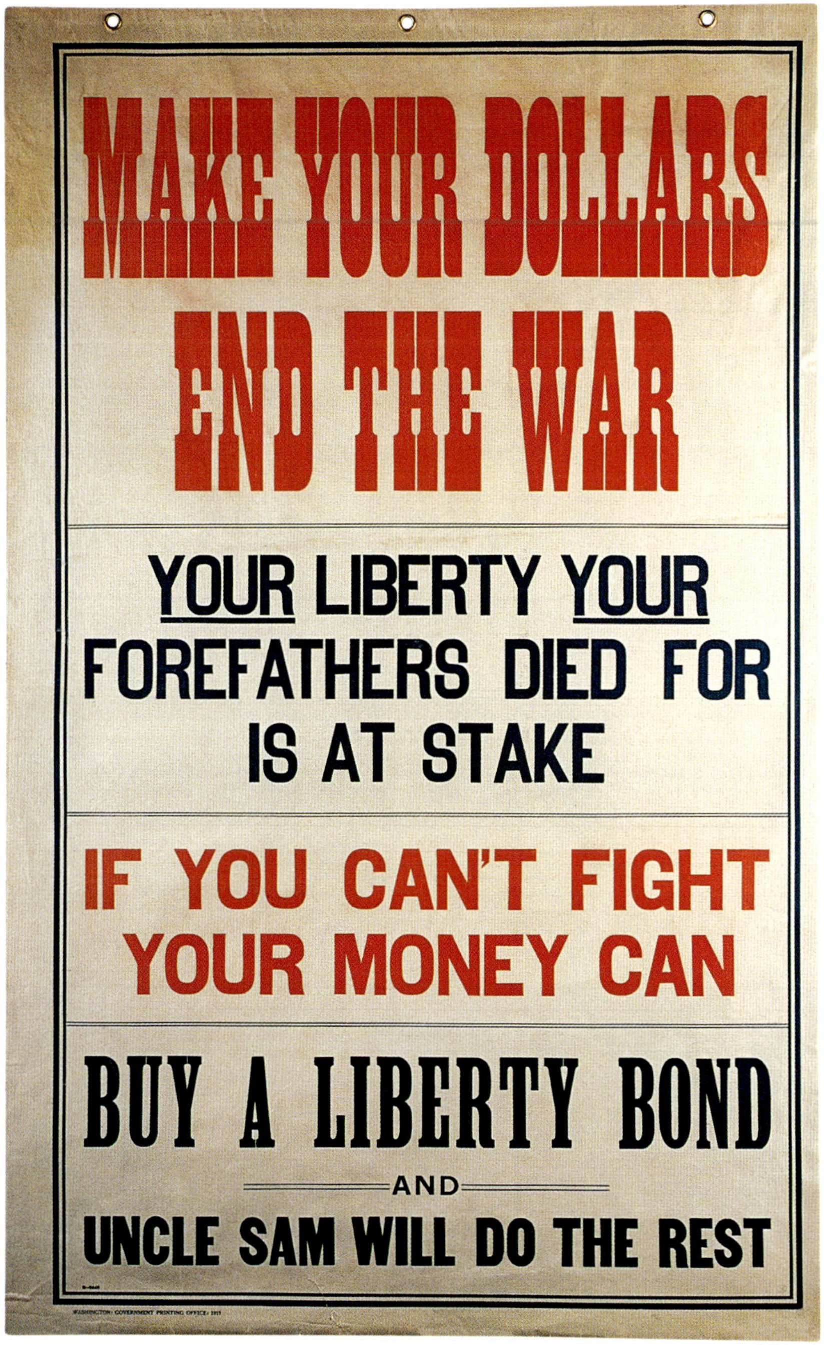

Make your dollars end the war, unsigned, 24" x 38", Government Printing Office, Washington, D.C., 1917. $100-$150.

(Italian) *Nel vostro stesso interesse*, unsigned, 21" x 28", no printer. $100-$150.

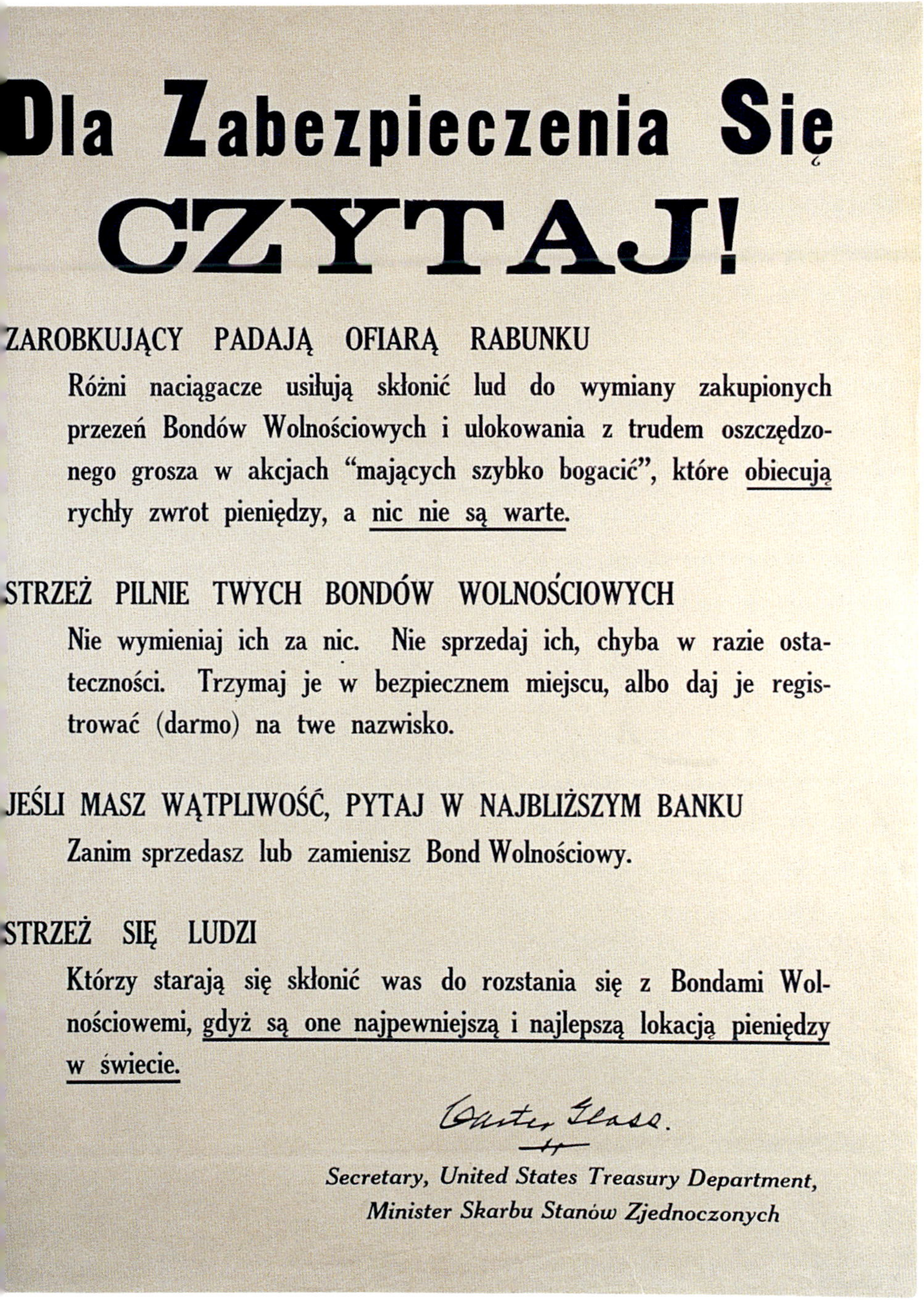

Dla zabezpieczenia sie Czytaj!, unsigned, 21" x 28", no printer. $100-$150.

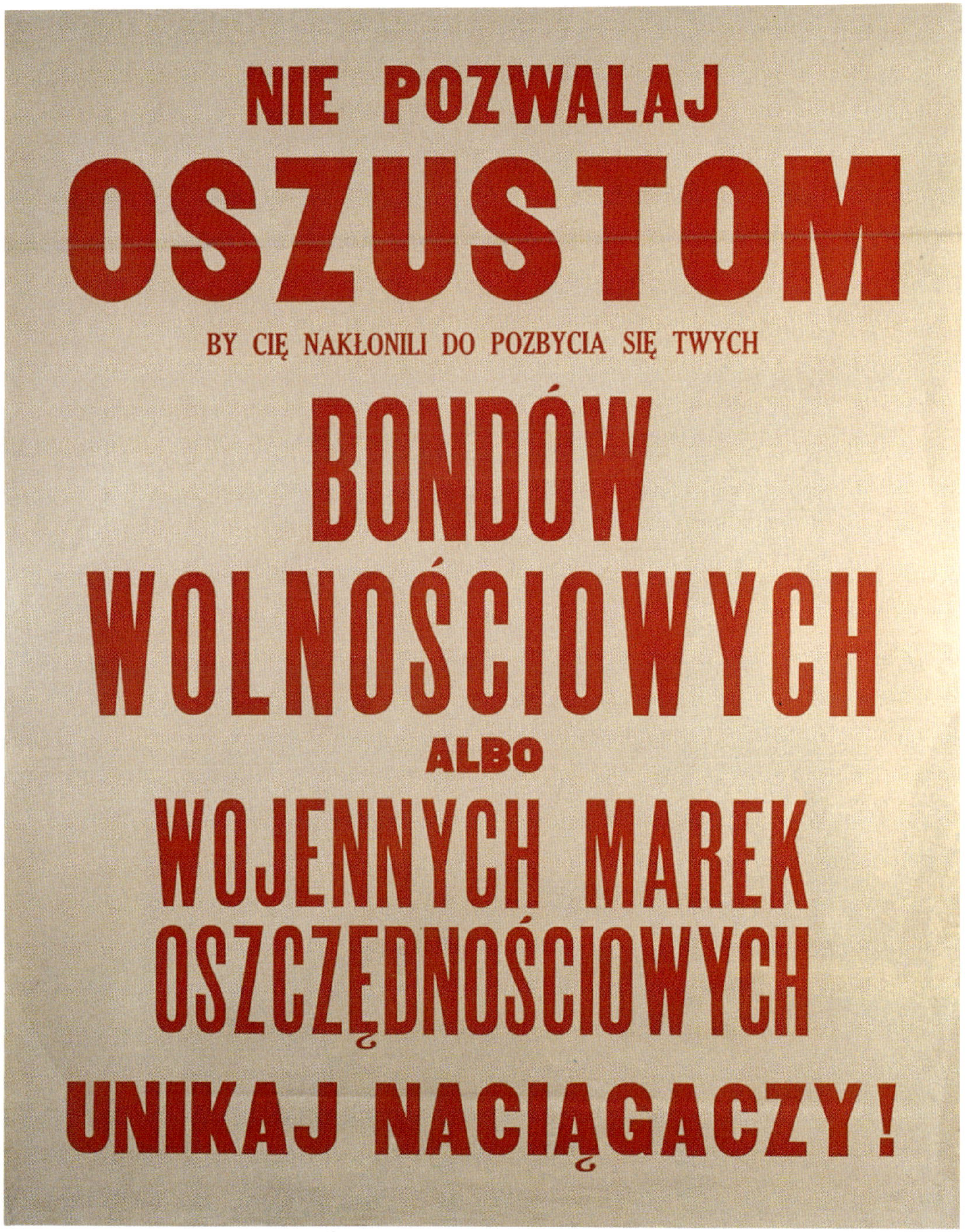

(Polish) *Nie pozwalaj oszustom*, unsigned, 21" x 28", no printer. $100-$150.

(Hungarian) *Magyararorszagnak*, unsigned, 28" x 42", no printer. $100-$150.

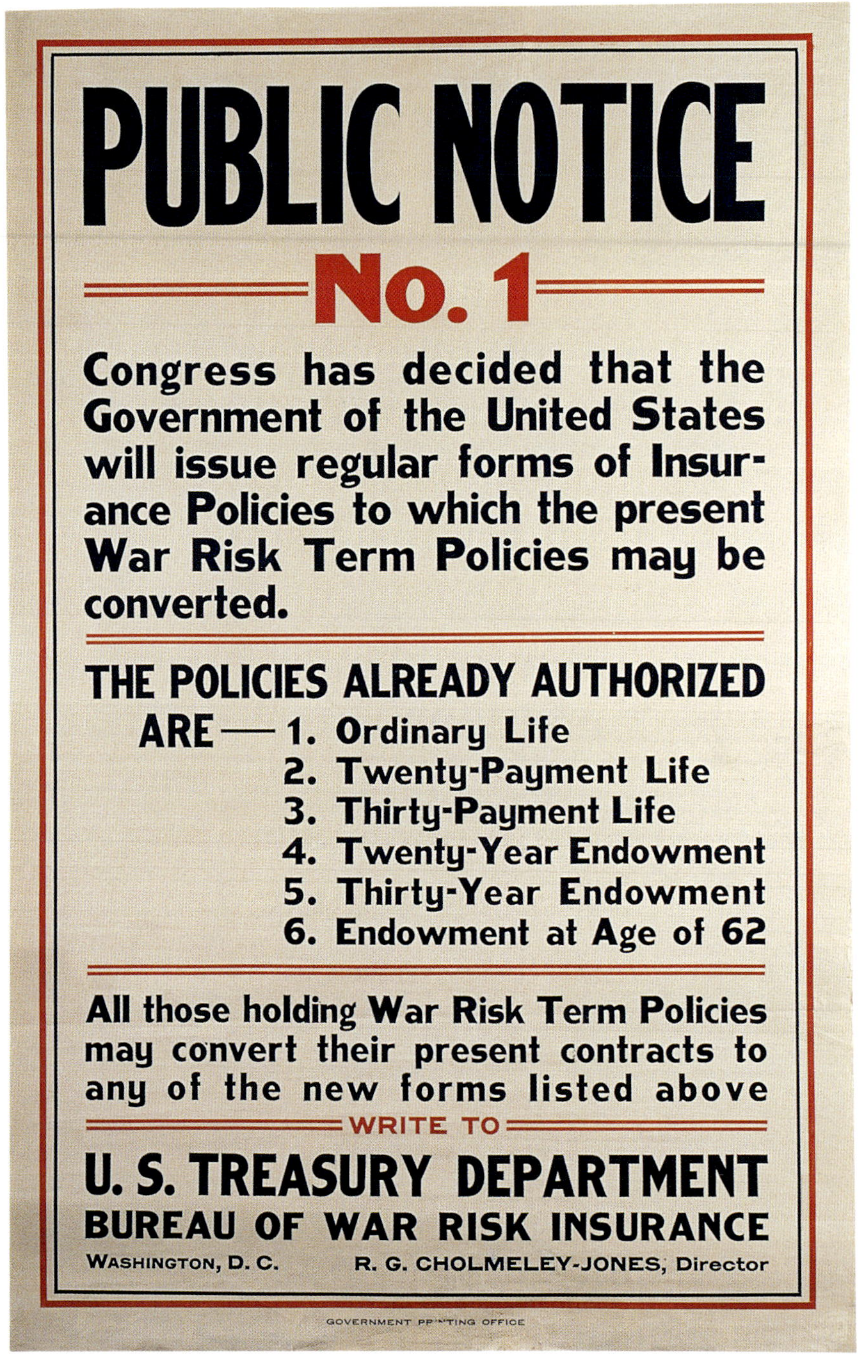

Public notice No. 1, unsigned, 21" x 32", U. S. Treasury Department, Bureau of War Risk Insurance, Government Printing Office, Washington, D.C. $100-$150.

War Savings Stamps

Is liberty worth 25 cents to you?, unsigned, 28" x 42", War Savings Stamps, no printer. $600-750. *Courtesy of Swann Galleries.*

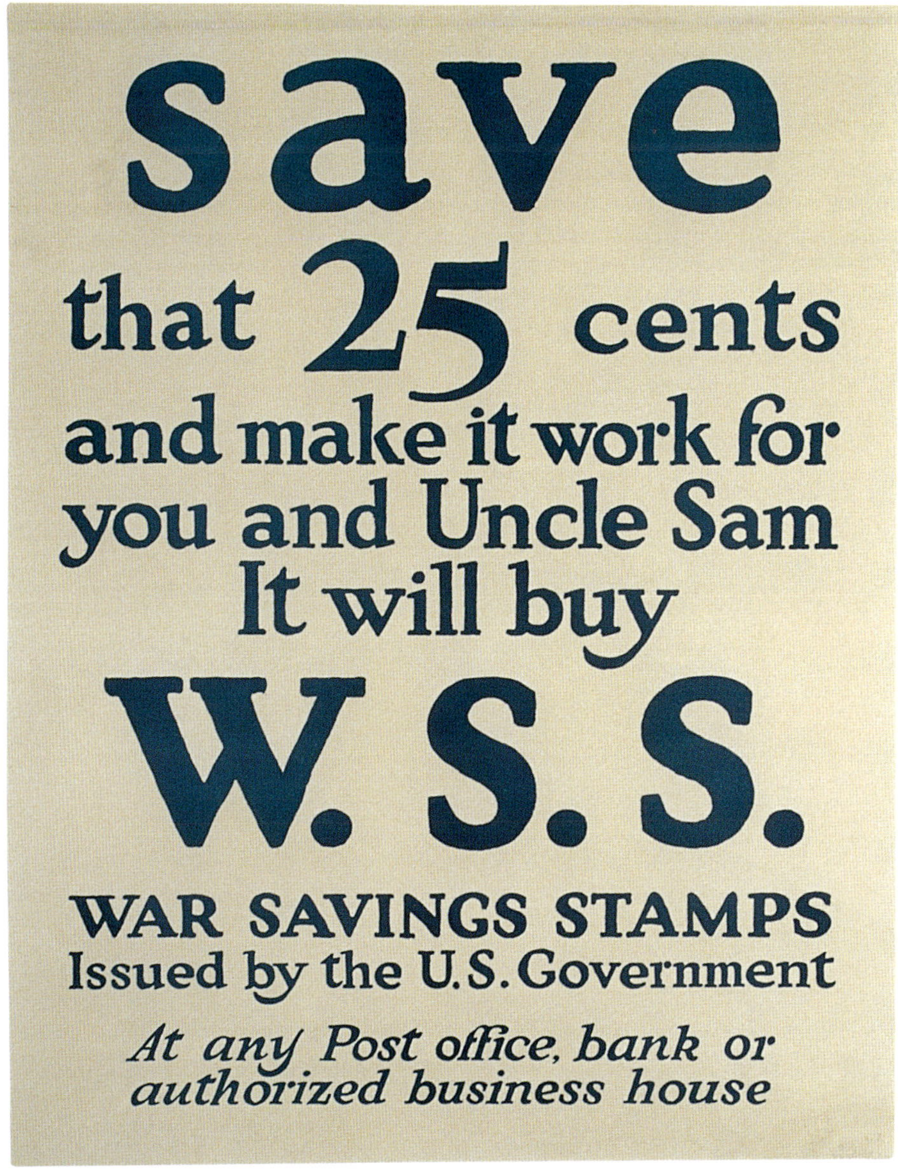

Save that 25 cents, unsigned, 14" x 18", War Savings Stamps, no printer. $50-$75.

Save-buy-for victory, unsigned, 15.5" x 22", War Savings Stamps, no printer. $50-$75.

"Stamp" it out, T. O. McGill, 13.5" x 18", War Savings Stamps, no printer. $75-$100.

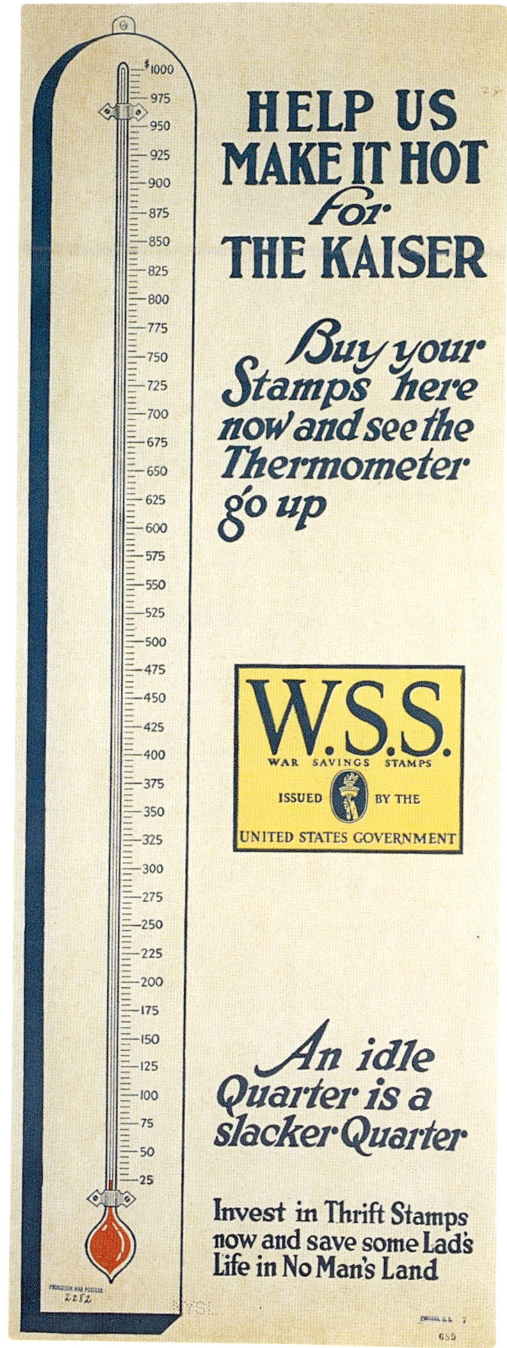

Help us make it hot for the Kaiser, unsigned, 11" x 28", War Savings Stamps, no printer. $100-$150. On thin card stock.

Stamp! Stamp!! Stamp!!!, T. O. McGill, 13.5" x 18", War Savings Stamps, no printer. $75-$100.

My soldier, H. R. Green, 14" x 22", War Savings Stamps, The Matthews-Northrup Works, Buffalo, Cleveland, and New York. $100-$150. Also found in 30" x 40" format for Third Liberty Loan, value $200-$300.

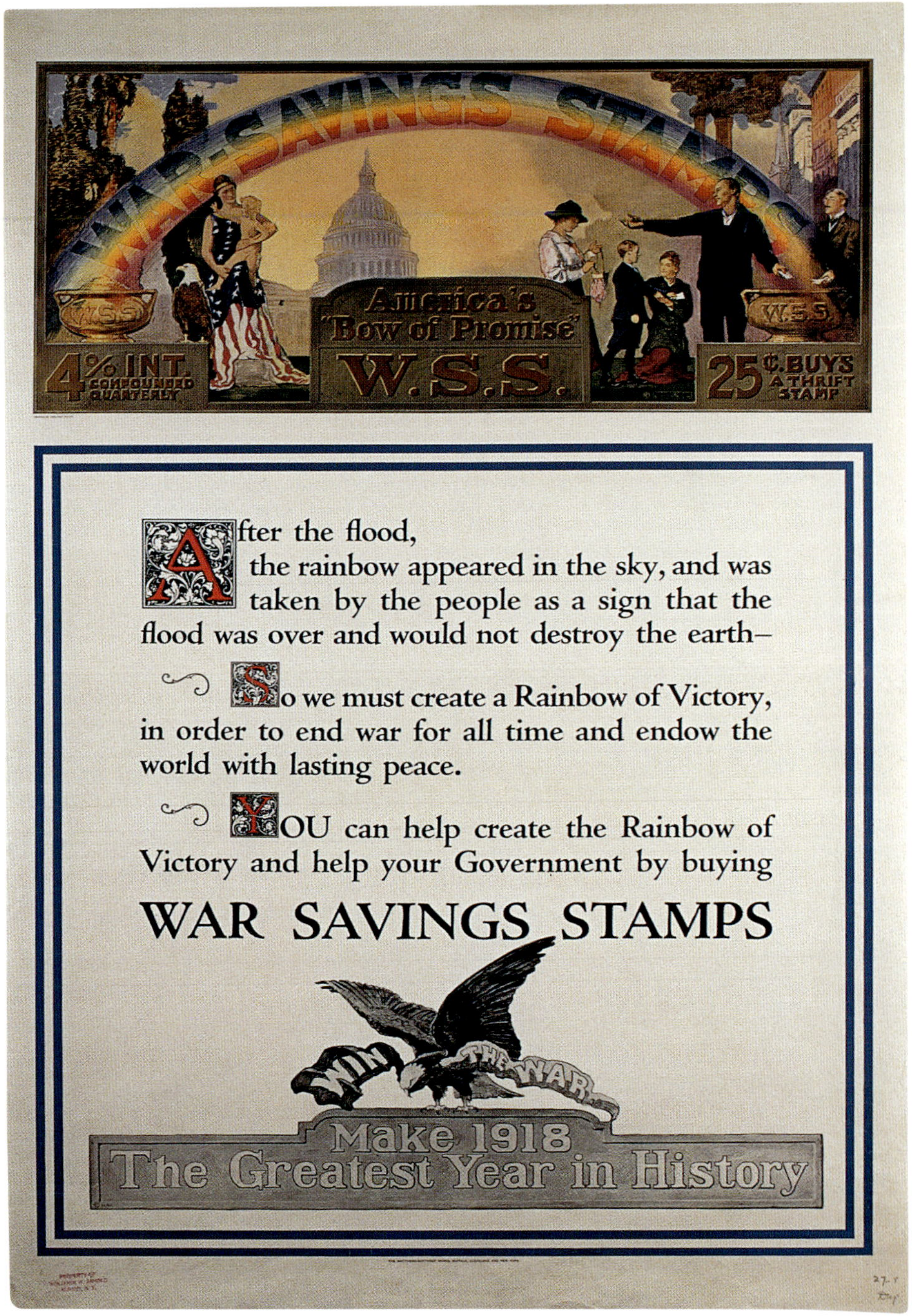

America's "Bow of Promise", Urquhart Wilcox, 24.5" x 38", War Savings Stamps, The Matthews-Northrup Works, Buffalo, Cleveland and New York. $150-$200. Uncommon.

Help them, Casper Emerson, 20" x 30", War Savings Stamps, American Litho Co., New York. $200-$300.

To the folk back home, C. Le Roy Baldridge, 20" x 30", Victory Liberty Loan, Robert Gair Co., Brooklyn, New York. $100-$150.

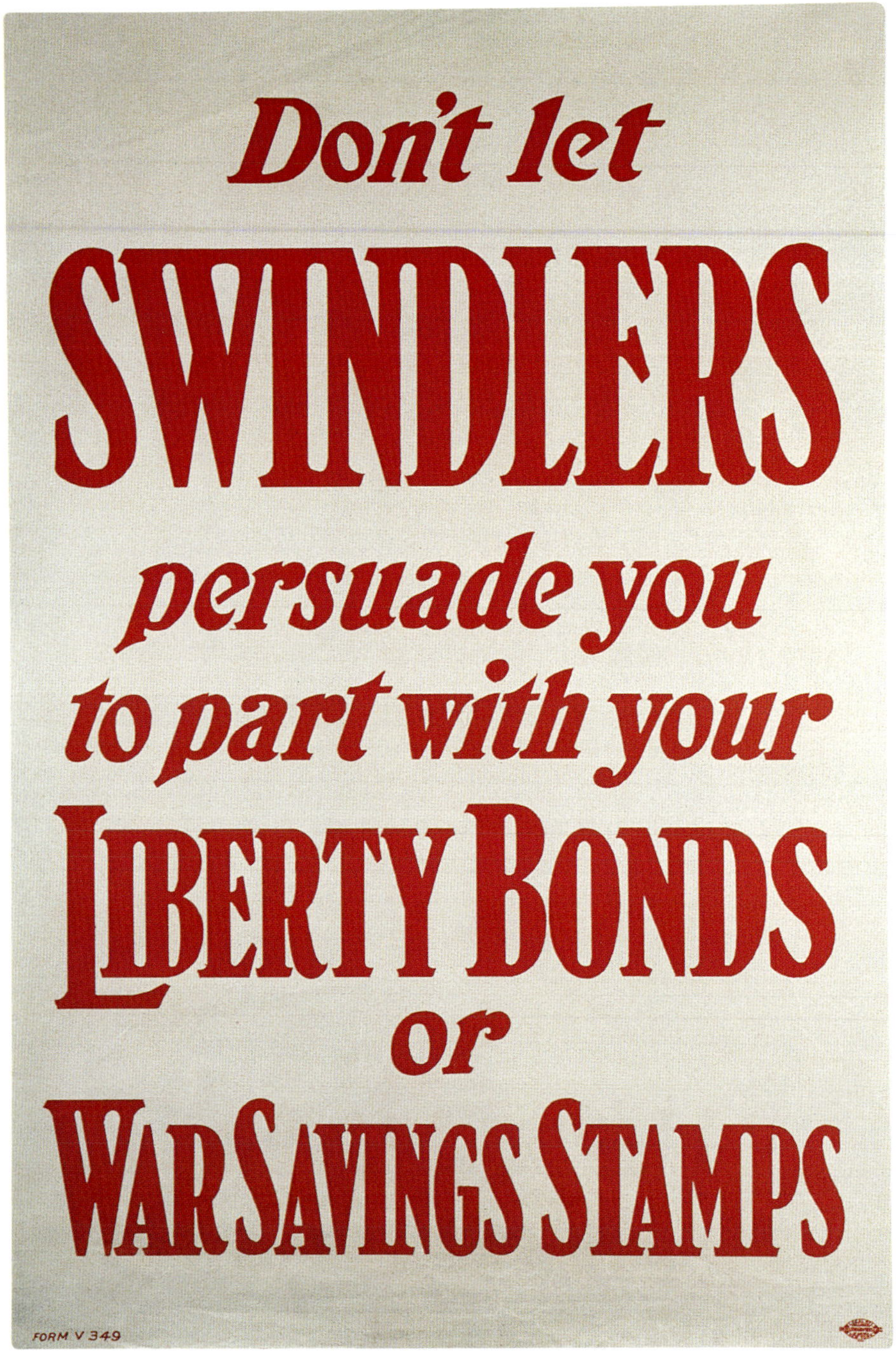

Don't let swindlers persuade you, unsigned, 20" x 30", Liberty Bonds, War Savings Stamps, no printer. $100-$150.

I have never seen my daddy, unsigned, 22" x 28", War Savings Stamps, The Matthews Northrup Works, Buffalo, Cleveland, and New York. $200-$300. Scarce.

Save your child from autocracy, Herbert Paus, 30" x 40", War Savings Stamps, United States Printing and Litho Co., New York. $200-$300. Also seen in 20" x 30" size, value $150-$200.

Boys and girls! You can help your Uncle Sam, James Montgomery Flagg, 30" x 40, War Savings Stamps, American Litho Co., New York. $300-$450. Also seen in 20" x 30" size, value $200-$300.

Share in the victory, Haskell Coffin, 28" x 42", War Saving Stamps, no printer. $300-$450. Also seen in 20" x 30" size, value $200-$300.

Joan of Arc saved France, Haskell Coffin, 20" x 30", War Savings Stamps, United States Printing and Litho Co., New York. $200-$300. Also seen in 30" x 40" size, value $300-$450.

Help him win by saving and serving, unsigned, 20" x 30", War Savings Stamps, American Litho Co., New York. $150-$200. Fine imagery of General Pershing.

Keep him free, Charles Livingston Bull, 20" x 30", War Saving Stamps, Ketterlinus, Philadelphia. $300-$450.

Your war savings pledge, unsigned, 21" x 33", War Savings Stamps, no printer. $100-$150.

The Browning Uncle Sam's official machine gun, unsigned, 20" x 28", Schulte Cigar Store Thrift Stamp Series, no printer. $600-$750. Very scarce privately printed war poster. *Courtesy of Robert Segel.*

United War Work Campaign

This home is helping our boys over there, unsigned, 7" x 10.5", United War Work Campaign, no printer. $50-$75. Small handbill format.

A message to the American people, unsigned, 14" x 22", United War Work Campaign, Y.W.C.A., no printer. $100-$150. Uncommon.

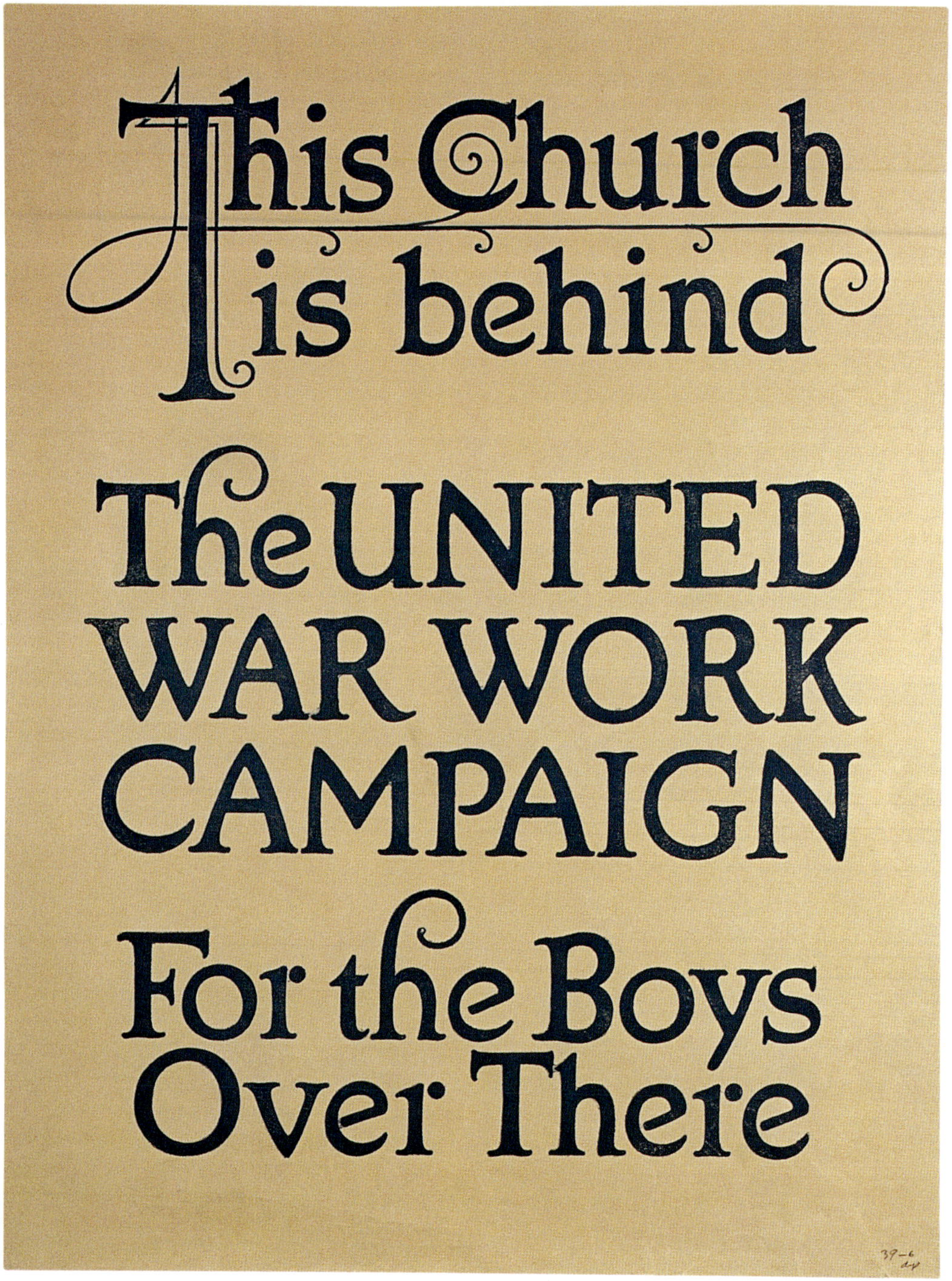

This church is behind the United War Work Campaign, unsigned, 19" x 25", United War Work Campaign, no printer. $50-$75.

Keep 'em smiling!, M. Leone Bracker, 28" x 42", War Camp Community Service, no printer. $100-$150. One of the most frequently seen larger posters.

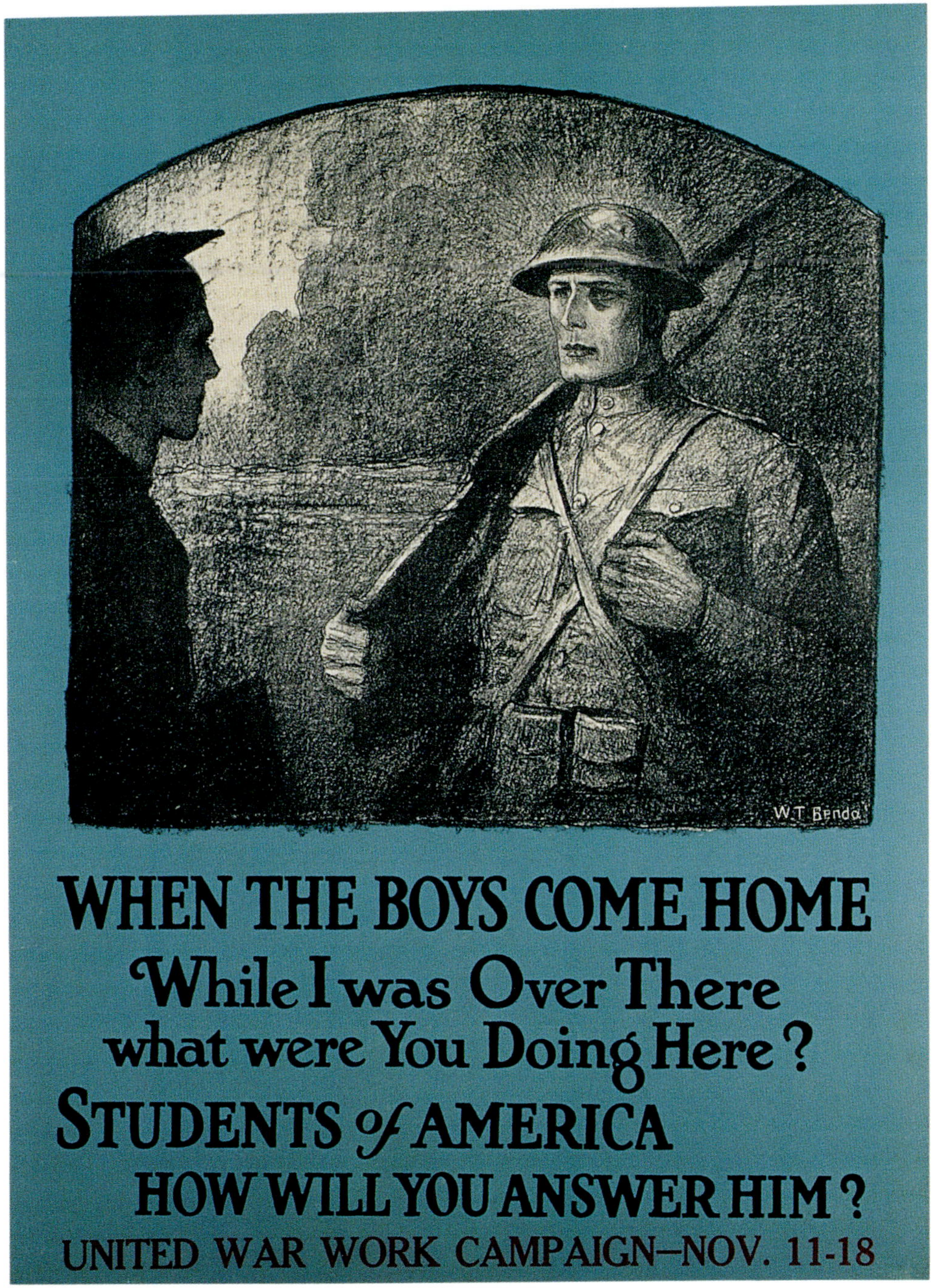

When the boys come home, W. T. Benda, 21" x 28", United War Work Campaign, no printer. $200-$300. Scarce.

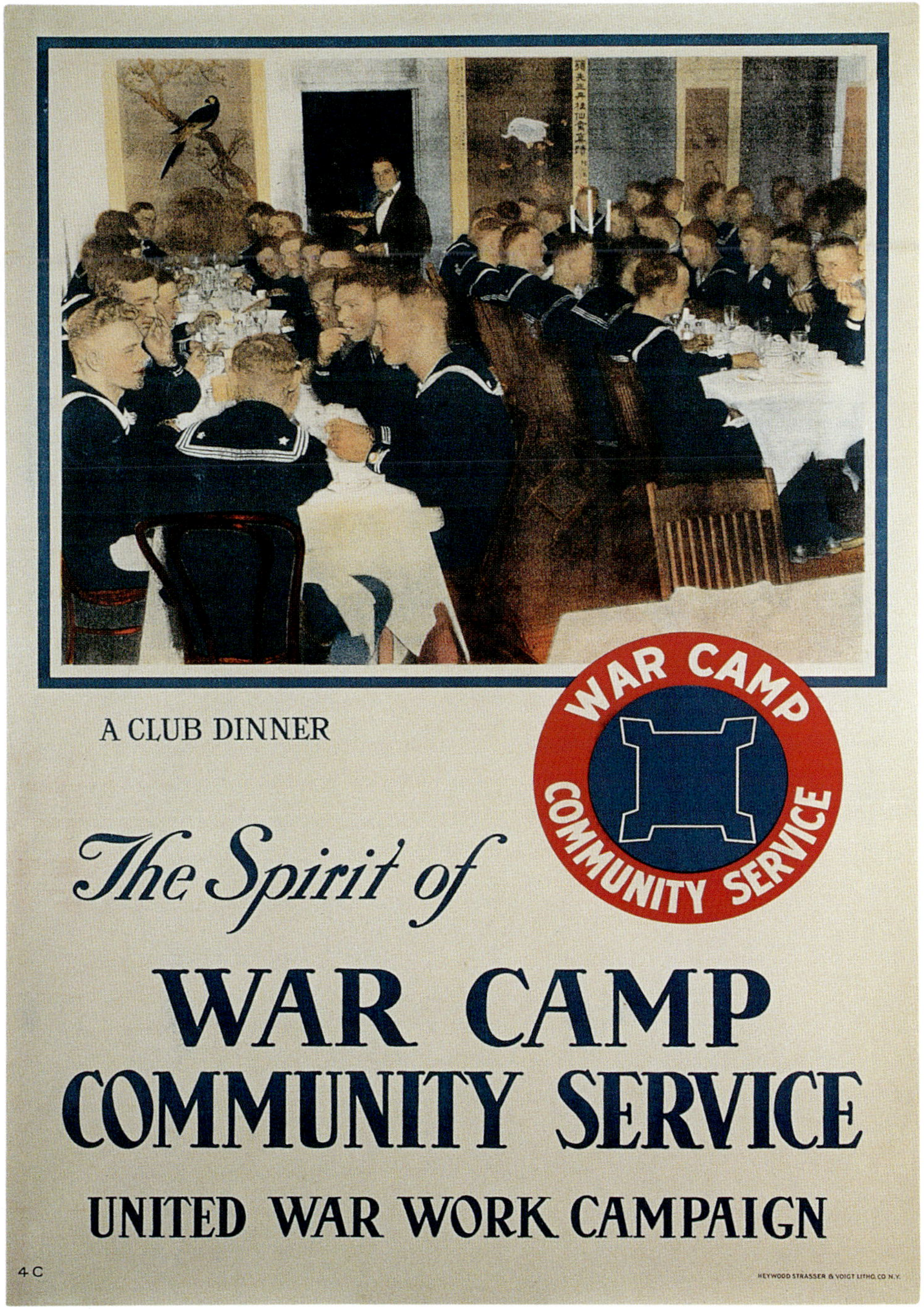

The Spirit of War Camp Community Service, a club dinner, unsigned, 20" x 30", War Camp Community Service, Heywood Strasser and Voigt Litho, New York. $100-$150. Several images found with this design.

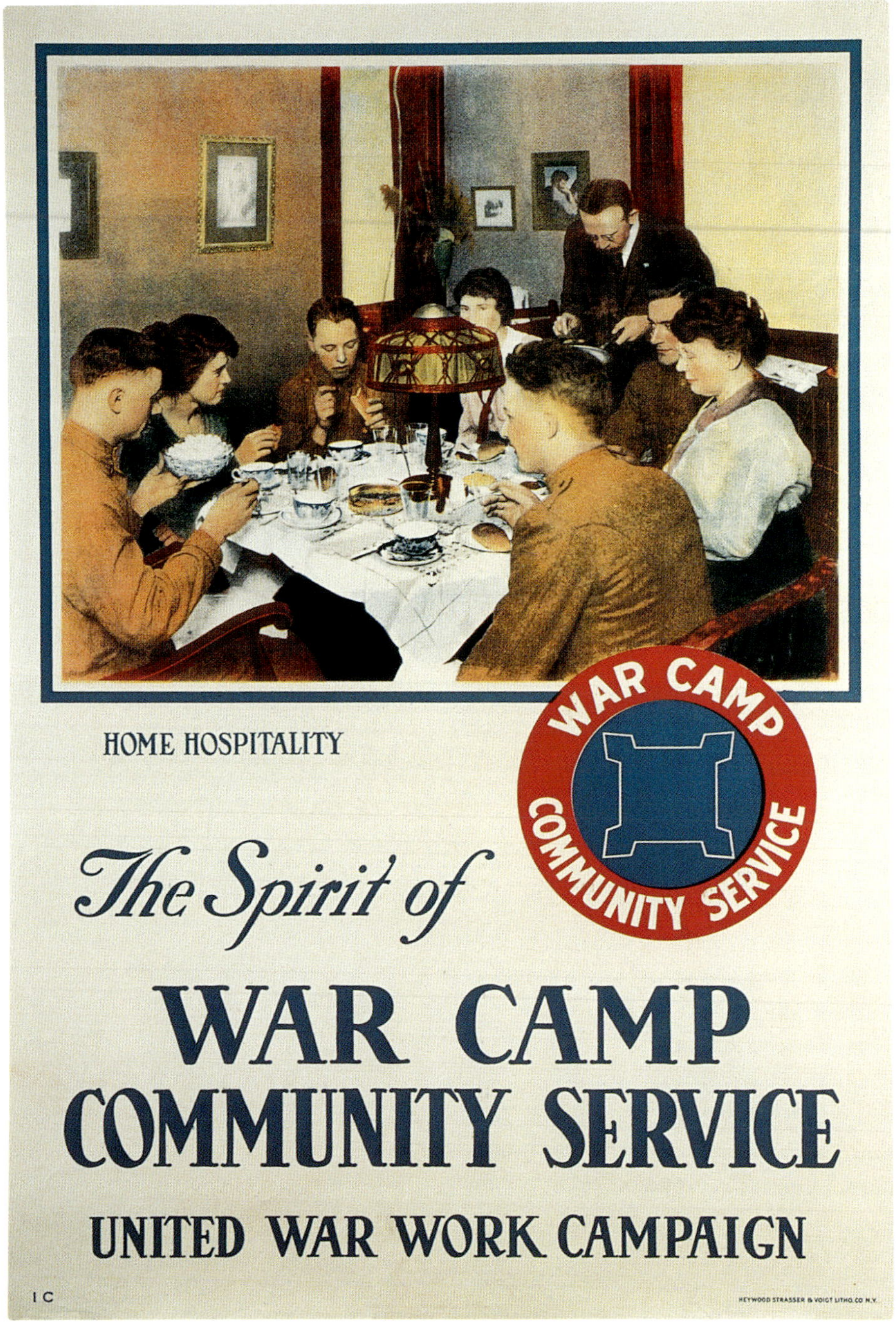

The Spirit of War Camp Community Service, home hospitality, unsigned, 20" x 30", War Camp Community Service, Heywood Strasser and Voigt Litho, New York. $100-$150.

The Spirit of War Camp Community Service, songs of today & yesterday, unsigned, 20" x 30", War Camp Community Service, Heywood Strasser and Voigt Litho, New York. $100-$150.

Four years in the fight, Jonas Lie, 28" x 42", United War Work Campaign, Strobridge Litho Co., Cincinnati and New York. $400-$550.

Every American boy should enroll in the Victory Boys, unsigned, 12.5" x 20.5", Victory Boys, no printer. $200-$300. On cardboard.

United we serve, unsigned, 20" x 30", United War Work Campaign, no printer. $75-$100.

American Red Cross

The first three!, Kidder, 20.5" x 27.5", American Red Cross, no printer. $100-$150.

All they ask is your old clothes, 21" x 28", American Red Cross, no printer. $100-$150.

What can you do?, unsigned, 28" x 41", American Red Cross, no printer. $200-$300.

Red Cross Christmas Roll Call, E. H. Blashfield, 19" x 28", American Red Cross, no printer. $150-$200.

Second Red Cross War Fund, W. F. Barclay, 22" x 32", American Red Cross, no printer. $150-$200.

There! In peace as in war, unsigned, 20" x 30", American Red Cross, no printer. $100-$150.

How much to save these little lives?, unsigned, 20.5" x 27.5", American Red Cross, no printer. $150-$200.

What are you doing to help?, Gordon Grant, 25" x 38", American Red Cross, no printer. $200-$300.

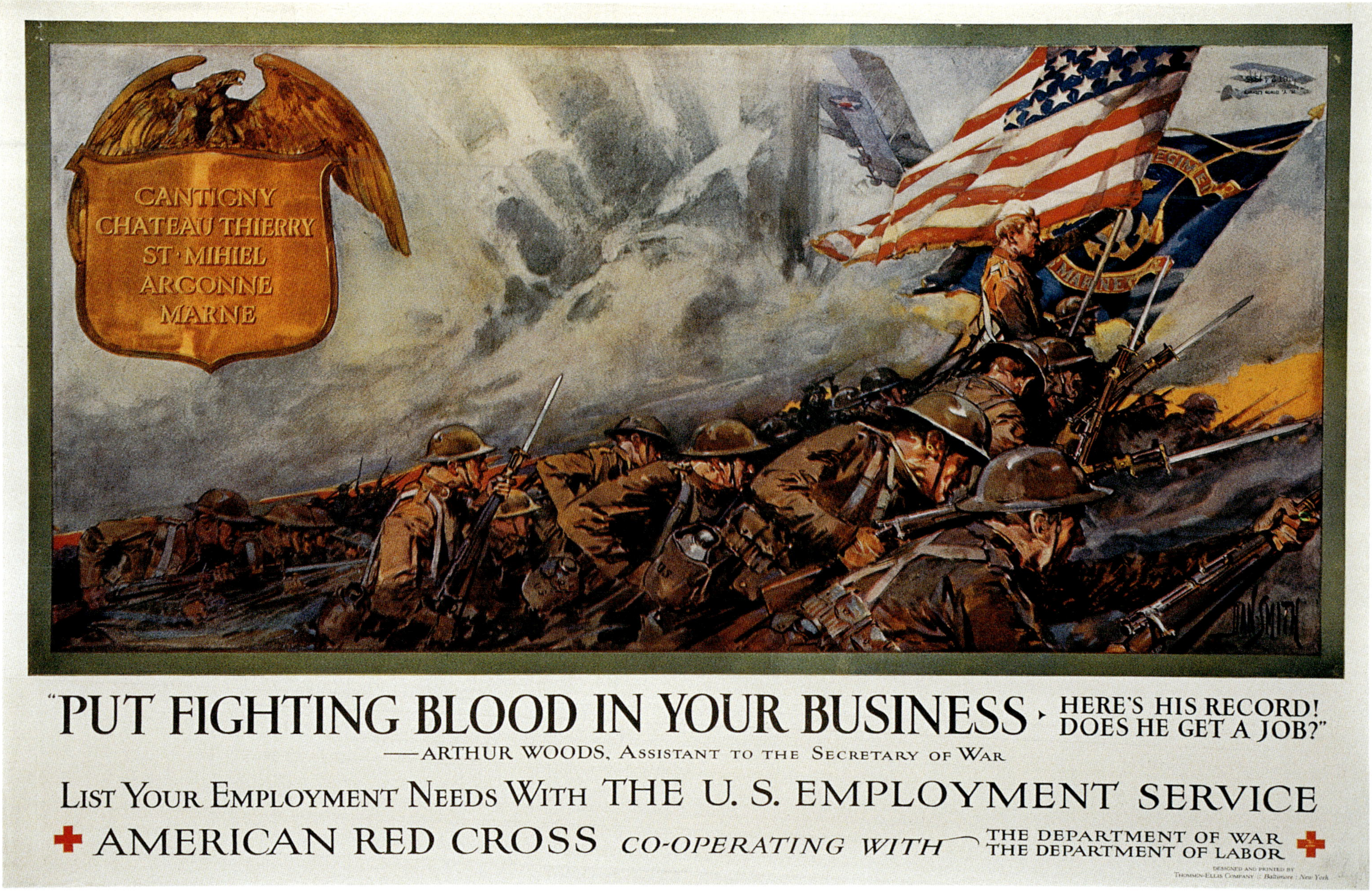

Put fighting blood in your business, Dan Smith, 19" x 28", American Red Cross, Thomsen-Ellis Co., Baltimore and New York. $150-$200. Fine image of U. S. Marines in action. Printed by halftone process.

Keep this hand of mercy at its work, P. G. Morgan, 21" x 27.5", American Red Cross, no printer. $100-$150.

Enrolls for National Service, unsigned, 20" x 30", American Red Cross, no printer. $100-$150.

The spirit of America, Howard Chandler Christy, 20" x 30", American Red Cross, Forbes Litho, Boston. $400-$550. Scarce.

Help your American Red Cross, unsigned, 30" x 46", American Red Cross, The Schilling Press Inc., New York. $300-$450.

I summon you to comradeship in the Red Cross, Harrison Fisher, 30" x 40", American Red Cross, American Litho Co., New York. $500-$650. One of the Fisher's few war posters, perhaps his best.

Untitled, Harrison Fisher, 21" x 25", American Red Cross, no printer. $200-$300. Also seen in 28" x 30" size with title *Have you answered the Red Cross Christmas Roll Call?*, value $300-$450.

At the service of all mankind, unsigned, 21" x 28", American Red Cross, Edwards and Deutsch Litho Co., Chicago. $150-$200.

Help the Red Cross, Herman Roeg, 20" x 30", American Red Cross, no printer. $150-$200.

He can win!, Dan Smith, 19" x 27", American Red Cross, Thomsen-Ellis Co., Baltimore and New York. $150-$200.

Hold up your end!, W. B. King, 21" x 28", American Red Cross, no printer. $150-$200.

You can help, W. T. Benda, 20" x 30", American Red Cross, American Litho Co., New York. $150-$200.

We belong 100% strong, unsigned, 17" x 23.5", American Red Cross, no printer. $50-$75.

The comforter, Gordon Grant, 18" x 24", American Red Cross, no printer. $100-$150.

Make our American Red Cross in peace as in war, unsigned, 20" x 30", American Red Cross, no printer. $100-$150.

10,000,000 members by Christmas, C. B. Falls, 20" x 30", American Red Cross, no printer. $150-$200.

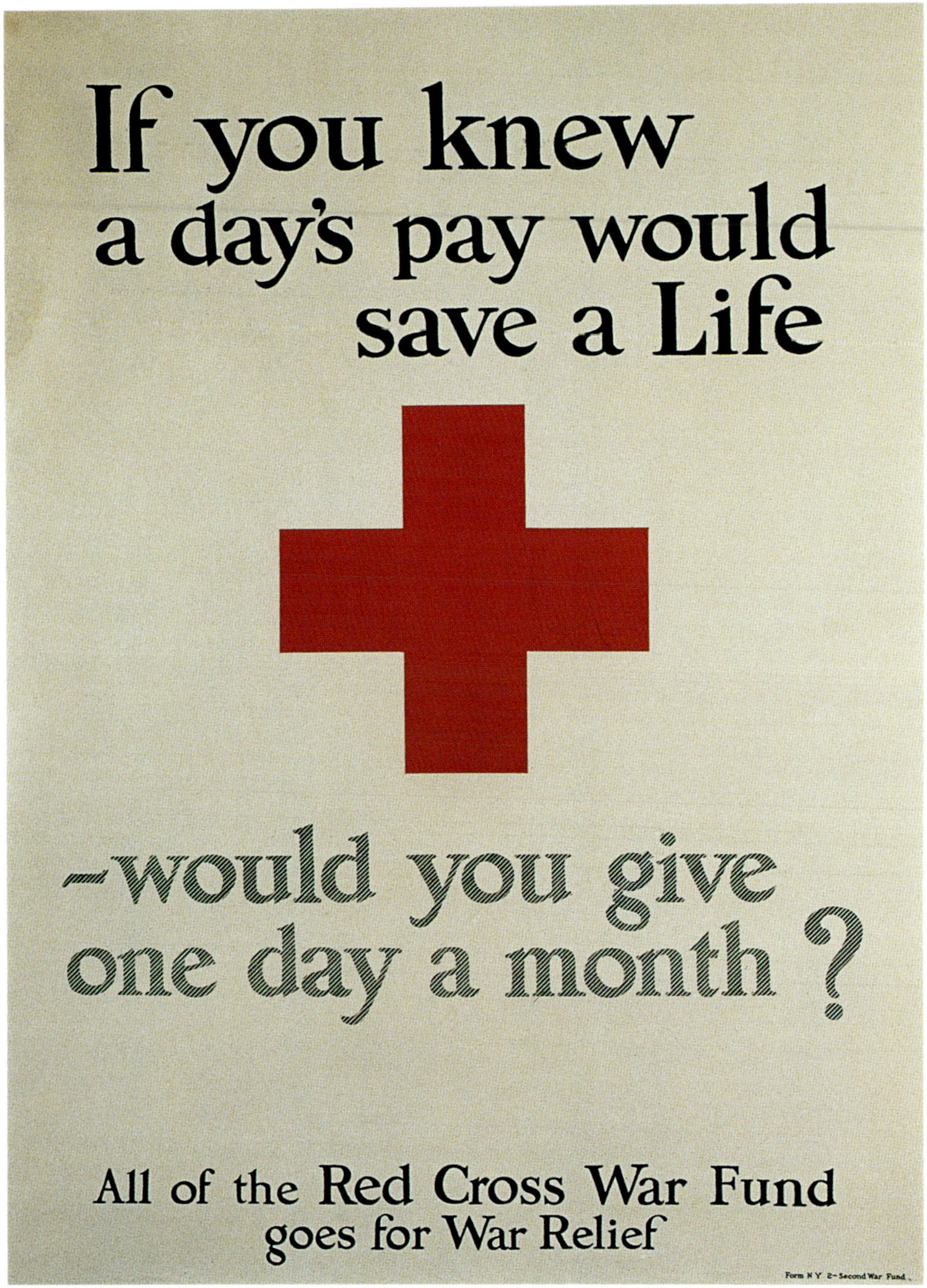

If you knew a day's pay would save a life, unsigned, 20.5" x 27", American Red Cross, no printer. $50-$75.

Answer the Red Cross Christmas Roll Call, Ray Greenleaf, 20" x 30", American Red Cross, Niagara Litho Co., Buffalo, New York. $100-$150.

The greatest mother in the world, A. E. Foringer, 21" x 28", American Red Cross, no printer. $100-$150. Also seen in 30" x 40" format, value $200-$300. Relatively common but popular classic.

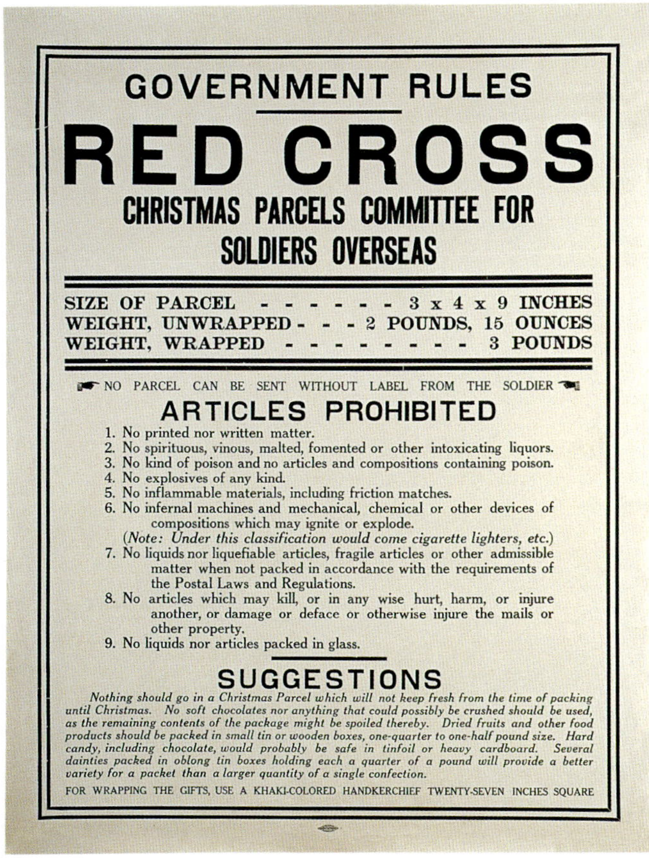

Red Cross Christmas parcels, unsigned, 22" x 28" American Red Cross, no printer. $75-$100.

They fight for you protect them, W. G. Sesser, 27.5" x 41", American Red Cross, Latham Litho. $200-$300.

Make good the promise, unsigned, 8.5" x 20.5", American Red Cross, no printer. $50-$75. Gummed at sides for pasting in window.

Third Red Cross Roll Call, Haskell Coffin, 20" x 30", American Red Cross, American Litho Co., New York. $200-$300.

Have you a Red Cross service flag?, Jessie Wilcox Smith, 21" x 28", American Red Cross, Forbes, Boston. $200-$300. Her only war poster, quite popular.

Y.M.C.A.

War-zone home for our boys "overthere", John F. Butler, 23.5" x 38", Y.M.C.A., Globe Litho Co., New York. $150-$200.

Wilson, Taft, Roosevelt and our other national leaders, John F. Butler, 24" x 38", Y.M.C.A., Globe Litho Co., New York. $150-$200.

Workers lend your strength to the Red Triangle, Gil Spear, 20" x 27", Y.M.C.A., no printer. $150-$200.

Big men wanted, Stockton Mulford, 14" x 22", Y.M.C.A., Robert Gair Co., Brooklyn, New York. $100-$150.

A sense of obligation, unclear signature, 22" x 32", Y.M.C.A. and United War Work Campaign, Alco Gravure Inc., New York. $100-$150. On low quality tan paper.

His home over there, Albert Herter, 27" x 42", Y.M.C.A., no printer. $150-$200.

One of the thousand Y.M.C.A. girls in France, Neysa McMein, 27" x 42", Y.M.C.A., no printer. $400-$550. Lovely and scarce.

Y.W.C.A.

The girl on the land serves the nation's need, Edward Penfield, 25" x 29.5", Y.W.C.A., United States Printing and Litho Co., New York. $750-$1000. *Courtesy of Swann Galleries.*

Soldiers-sailors and women guests, Walter Tittle, 28" x 39", Y.W.C.A., Gravure Co., New York. $150-$200.

Mothers! Wives! Friends! Of soldiers and sailors, Baldwin, 21" x 32", Y.W.C.A., no printer. $150-$200.

Girlhood calls for wartime training, W. T. Benda, 20.5" x 30.5", Y.W.C.A., no printer. $150-$200.

In service for the girls of the world, Neysa McMein, 20" x 30", Y.W.C.A., American Litho Co., New York. $150-$200.

Stand behind the country's girlhood, W. T. Benda, 20" x 30", Y.W.C.A., no printer. $150-$200.

For every fighter a women worker, Adolph Triedler, 30" x 40", Y.W.C.A., American Litho Co., New York. $400-$550.

For every fighter a women worker, Ernest Hamlin Baker, 27" x 41", Y.W.C.A. and United War Work Campaign, United States Printing and Litho Co., New York. $300-$450.

Remember the girl behind the man behind the gun, signed M. B., 20.5" x 29", Y.W.C.A. War Work Council, no printer. $200-$300.

The girl reserves of the Y.W.C.A., Poucher, 21" x 28", Y.W.C.A., The U. S. Printing and Lithograph Co., New York. $750-$1000. Very rarely seen.

Back our girls over there, Clarence Underwood, 21" x 28", Y.W.C.A., United War Work Campaign, no printer. $200-$300.

Tributes and Relief

Vive La France!, James Montgomery Flagg, 28" x 40", Allied Tribute To France, Carey Print Litho Co., New York, $750-$1000. Very scarce. *Courtesy of Swann Galleries.*

Side by side-Britannia!, James Montgomery Flagg, 20" x 27", Britain's Day, no printer. $600-$750. *Courtesy of Swann Galleries.*

America's tribute to Britain, F. G. Cooper, 20" x 30", America's Tribute to Britain, Marchbanks Press, New York. $400-$550. Printed by color woodcut process, unusual fine art style poster.

Britain's Day, December 7, 1918, unsigned, 27" x 38.5", America's Tribute to Britain, Carey Print Litho Co., New York. $400-$550. Uncommon.

Avez vous place dans votre coeur pour nous?, Walter De Maris, 20" x 30", Fatherless Children of France Inc., American Litho Co., New York. $200-$300.

Stage Women's War Relief, James Montgomery Flagg, 22" x 30", Stage Woman's War Relief, American Litho Co., New York. $1500-$2000. Rare. *Courtesy of Swann Galleries.*

America's gift to France, Albert Sterner, 20" x 30", National Committee of America's Gift to France, American Litho Co., New York. $200-$300.

Where the victims are, unsigned, 21" x 28", American Committee for Relief in the Near East, no printer. $100-$150.

The American Ambulance in Russia, signed B., 28" x 41", Erie Litho Co., Erie, Pennsylvania. $600-$750. A number of different rare foreign posters are also seen overprinted for the American Ambulance Service.

They shall not perish, Douglas Volk, 26" x 40", American Committee for Relief in the Near East, American Litho Co., New York. $400-$550.

Lest we perish, E. F. Bottsbains, 20" x 28", American Committee for Relief in the Near East, Conwell Graphic Co., New York. $200-$300.

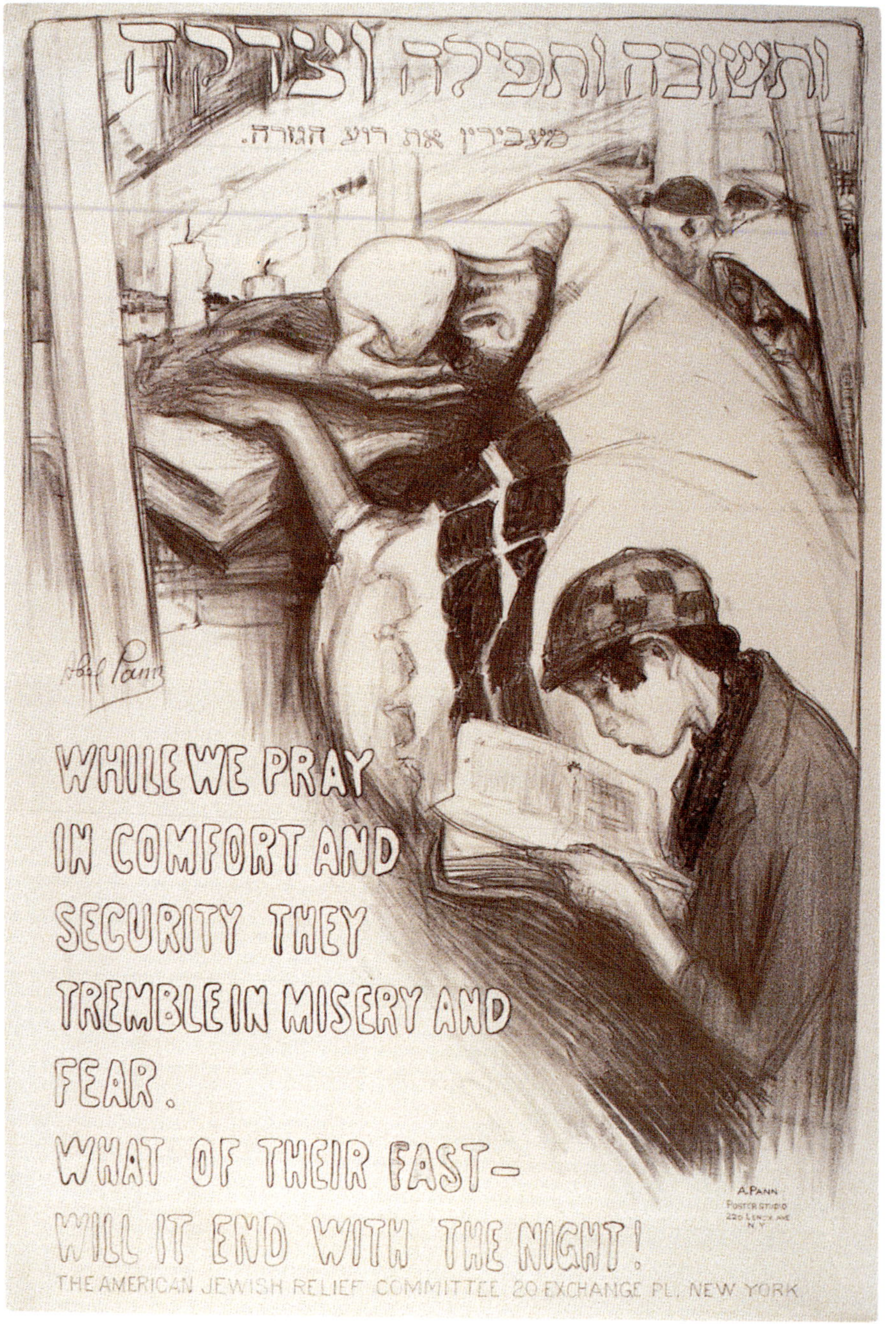

While we pray in comfort, Abel Pann, 25" x 38", American Jewish Relief Committee, A. Pann Poster Studio, New York, $1500-$2000. Very rare. *Courtesy of Swann Galleries*.

Share, Burke, 29.5" x 40", Jewish Relief Campaign, Sackett and Wilhelms, Brooklyn, New York. $2500-$3500. Rare and in much demand. *Courtesy of Swann Galleries.*

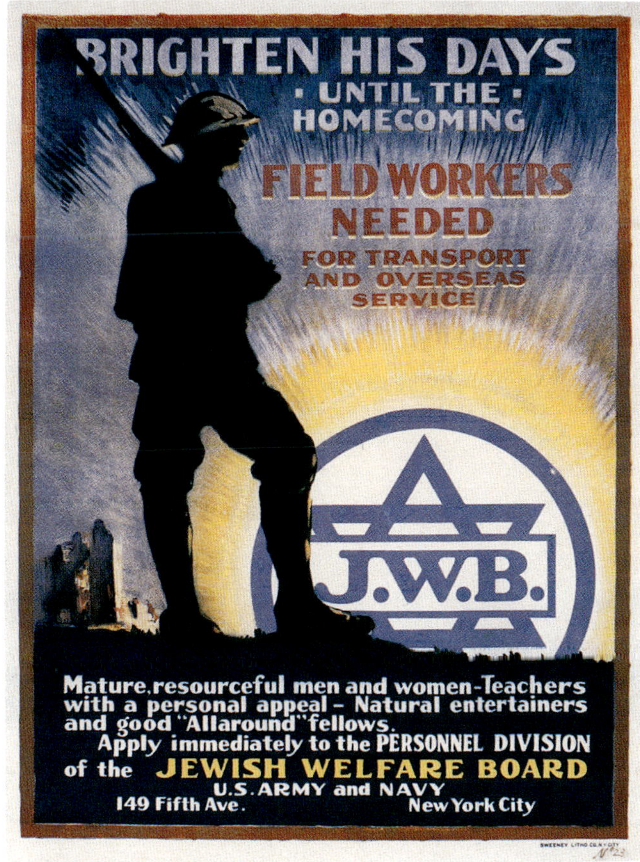

Brighten his days, unsigned, 21" x 28", Jewish Welfare Board, Sweeney Litho Co., New York, $1500-2000. Rare. *Courtesy of Swann Galleries.*

Jewish war sufferers shall they plead in vain?, Lou Mayer, 21" x 30", Latham Litho. $900-$1200. A close variant also published in Canada. *Courtesy of Swann Galleries.*

The Jewish Welfare Board, unsigned, 14" x 22", Jewish Welfare Board, Hegeman Print Co., New York, $1500-$2000. Rare. *Courtesy of Swann Galleries.*

Civilians, Sidney Reisenberg, 22" x 33", Jewish Welfare Board, Alco-Gravure Co., New York. $200-$300. The most common Jewish related war poster, printed on very low grade tan paper.

See him through, Burton Rice, 20" x 30", National Catholic War Council, Knights of Columbus, American Lithographic Co., New York. $150-$200.

Y. D. Club, A. W. Parsons, 30" x 40", Y. D. Club, no printer. $150-$200.

Wake Up America Day, James Montgomery Flagg, 28" x 41", Wake Up America Day, no printer. $1200-$1500. Very scarce. *Courtesy of Swann Galleries.*

Fight world famine, unsigned, 19" x 27.5", Boys Working Reserve, Thompson Ellis Co., Baltimore. $150-$200.

Knights of Columbus Three Million War Fund, Balfour Ker, 20" x 30", Knights of Columbus, no printer. $150-$200.

Send smokes to Sammy, James Montgomery Flagg, 12" x 17", Our Boys in France Tobacco Fund, no printer. $300-$450. Scarce.

Give to the American Chocolate Fund, Dotking, 21" x 27.5", American Chocolate Fund, Sackett and Wilhelms, New York. $500-$650. *Courtesy of Swann Galleries.*

Help him to help U. S.!, James Montgomery Flagg, 22.5" x 33", American Red Star Animal Relief, W. F. Powers Co. Litho, New York. $750-$1000.

Library and Books

They signal "send books," Holmes, 25" x 38.5", The Public Library, H. C. Miner Litho Co., New York. $300-$450.

Hey fellows! Your money brings the book we need, Sheridan, 20" x 30", American Library Association, American Lithograph Co., New York. $150-$200.

Yanks in Germany want more books, C. B. Falls, 28" x 31", American Library Association, no printer. $500-$650. Scarce.

Knowledge wins, Dan Smith, 19" x 28", American Library Association, Thompson Ellis Co., Baltimore. $300-$450. Printed by halftone process.

Books wanted, C. B. Falls, 27.5" x 40.5", no printer. $500-$650.

Official War Films

Official United States War Films, unsigned, 28.5" x 41", Official United States War Films, Hegeman Print Co., New York. $400-$550. *Courtesy of Swann Galleries.*

If it's worth living under it's worth fighting for, Guenther, 28" x 41", Associated Motion Picture Advertisers, no printer. $300-$450.

It's up to you. Schenck, 28" x 42", Associated Motion Picture Advertisers, Acme Litho Co. $750-$1000.

Great war film, our American boys in the European War, Victor Tardieu, 28" x 41", American Ambulance Field Service, United States Printing and Litho Co., New York. $400-$550.

If your soldier's hit, E. M. Gean Jackson, 28" x 41", Division of Films, Standard Litho Co., New York. $400-$550.

Official United States War Films, Stoner, 28" x 41", Official United States War Films, Alpha Litho, New York. $600-$750.

Postwar Readjustment

Back into "cits," and the American Legion, Ernest Hamlin Baker, 28" x 40.5", American Legion, Carey Print Litho, New York. $300-$450. *Courtesy of Swann Galleries.*

After the welcome home- a job!, E. M. Ashe, 28" x 41", U. S. Employment Service, Heywood Strasser and Voigt, New York. $400-$550.

The U. S. Employment Service, Gordon Grant, 14.5" x 22", U. S. Employment Service, Thomson Ellis Co., Baltimore. $150-$200.

First in war, first in peace, unsigned, 11" x 14", Service Series, No. 38, no printer. $50-$75. Part of a large series of small format posters, each with similar value.

Hold on to Uncle Sam's insurance, James Montgomery Flagg, 20" x 30", Forbes, Boston. $300-$450.

May 30, Harry S. Mueller, 11" x 14", Service Series, Memorial Day, no printer. $50-$75.

A chevron of honor, Gordon Grant, 11" x 14", Service Series, No. 37, no printer. $50-$75.

Down to earth, Gordon Grant and Walter Wilhelm, 11" x 14", Service Series, No. 41, no printer. $50-$75.

Canada

Your chums are fighting why aren't you?, unsigned, 25" x 38", Stone Litho Co. $300-$400. *Courtesy of Swann Galleries.*

Buy your Victory Bonds, unsigned, 39" x 53.5", Victory Bonds, no printer. $750-$1000. Canada's version of *I want you*.

Canadiens suivez l'example de Dollard des Ormeaux, unsigned, 24" x 36", Regiments Canadiens-Francais, no printer. $200-$300.

Oh please do! Daddy, Sampson, 24" x 36", Victory Bonds, WP-3. $200-$300.

Canada's grain cannot be sold, Malcolm Gibson, 24" x 36", Victory Bonds, WP-2. $200-$300. This and the following Canadian Victory Bond posters are found in both English and French titles, these variants have similar values.

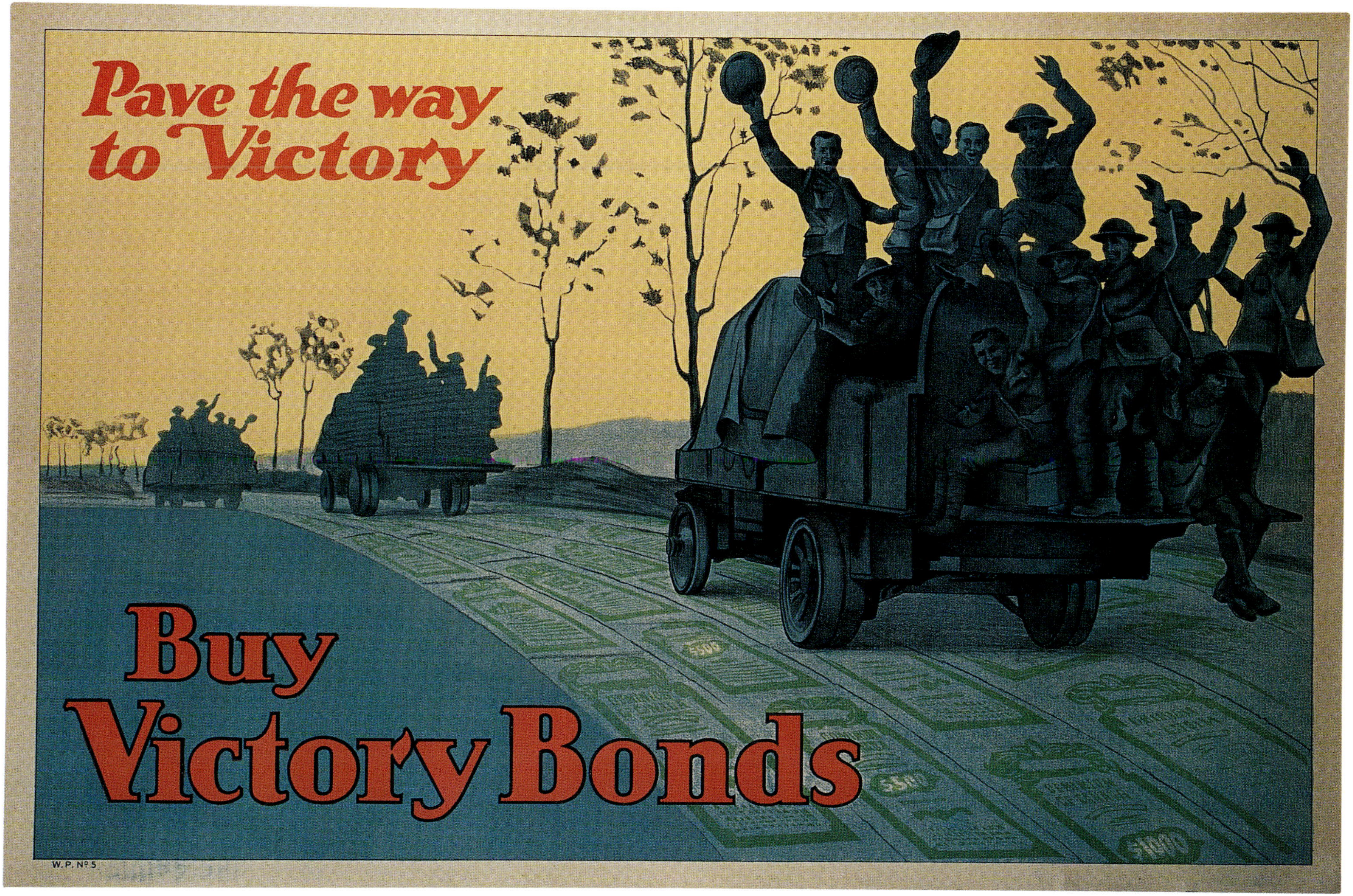

Pave the way to victory, unsigned, 24" x 36", Victory Bonds, WP-5. $200-$300.

Every dollar spent in Canada, unsigned, 24" x 36", Victory Bonds, WP-6. $200-$300.

Back him up!, unsigned, 24" x 36", Victory Bonds, WP-6. $200-$300.

Let us win the Prince of Wales' flag, unsigned, 24" x 36", Victory Bonds, WP-9. $150-$200.

For industrial expansion, Arthur Keelor, 23" x 36", Victory Bonds, WP-8. $300-$450. Very bold industrial image.

Bring him home with the Victory Loan, unsigned, 24" x 36", Victory Loan, WP-6. $200-$300.

Faith in Canada, unsigned, 24" x 36", Victory Bonds, WP-3. $200-$300.

Come On!, unsigned, 24" x 36", Victory Bonds, WP-5. $200-$300.

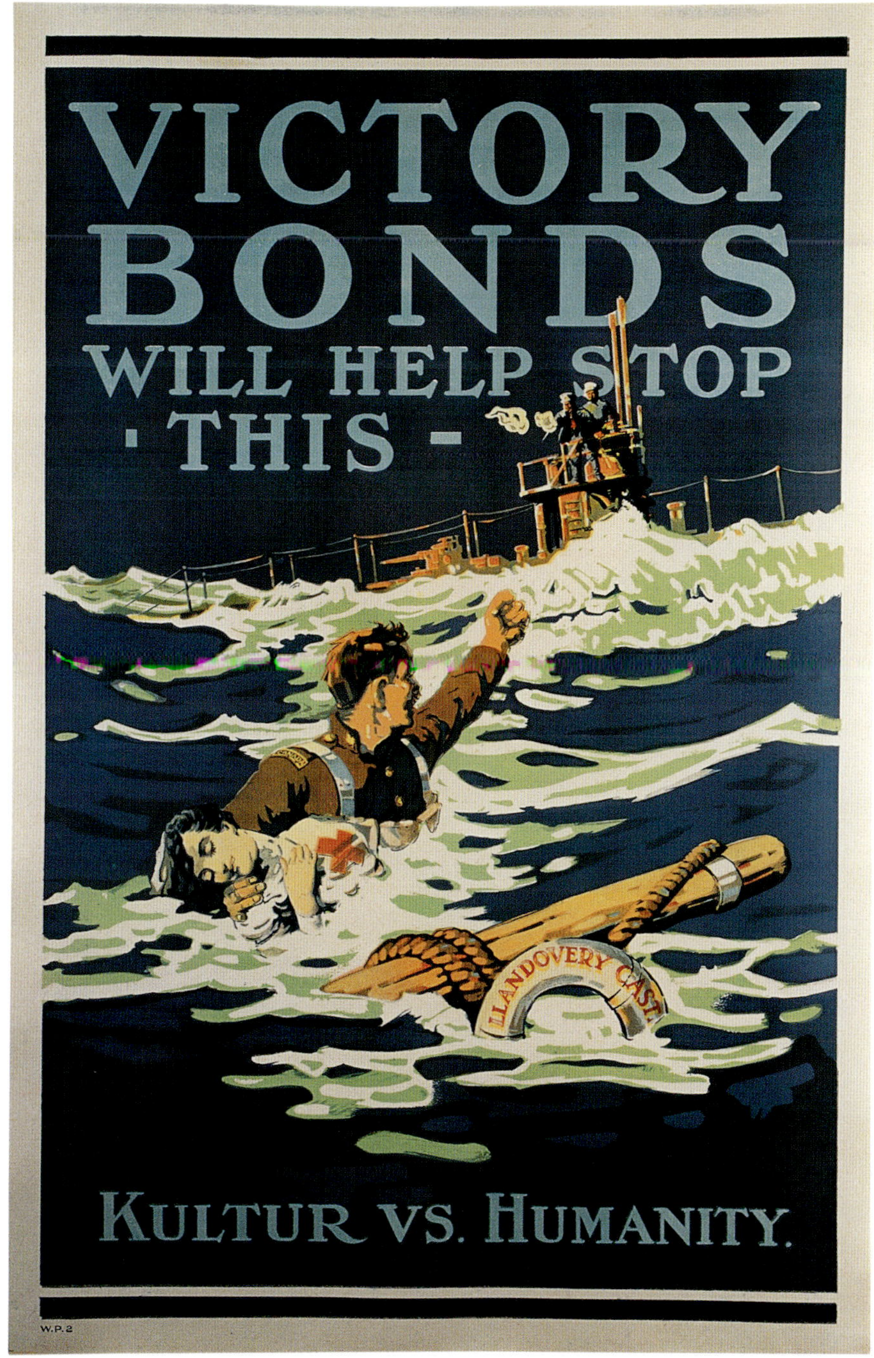

Victory Bonds will help stop this, unsigned, 24" x 36", Victory Bonds, WP-2. $200-$300. Depicts sinking of hospital ship Llandovery Castle.

Our best customer, but- he needs credit!, Malcolm Gibson, 24" x 36", Victory Bonds, WP-3. $200-$300.

Doing my bit four years, unsigned, 23" x 36", Victory Bonds, WP-4. $200-$300.

Rien a faire, Malcolm Gibson, 34" x 36", Victory Bond, WP-4. $300-$450. Very unusual and subtle, perhaps the finest artwork of the Victory Bond series.

They serve France, how can I serve Canada?, unsigned, 24" x 36", Victory Bonds, WP-7. $200-$300.

Yours not to do and die, unsigned, 24" x 36", Victory Bonds, WP-8. $200-$300.

Humanity knows no creed, Lou Mayer, 21" x 28", Canadian Jewish War Relief, Litho-Print, Toronto. $1500-2000. Rare. *Courtesy of Swann Galleries.*

Are you one of Kitchener's own?, 27" x 41", Army Recruiting, Montreal Litho Co. Ltd., Montreal. $400-$550.

Great Britain

Come lad slip across and help, unsigned, 40" x 50", Parliamentary Recruiting Committee, David Allen and Sons, London. $400-$550. *Courtesy of Swann Galleries.*

Boys come over here, you're wanted, unsigned, 40" x 50", Parliamentary Recruiting Committee, David Allen and Sons, London. $400-$550. *Courtesy of Swann Galleries.*

Step into your place, unsigned, 20" x 30", Parliamentary Recruiting Committee, No. 104, David Allen and Sons, Harrow. $200-$300. *Courtesy of Swann Galleries.*

Irishmen avenge the Lusitania, signed W. E. J., 20" x 30", Central Council for Organisation of Recruiting in Ireland, John Shuley, Dublin. $1200-$1500. Very scarce and desirable. *Courtesy of Swann Galleries.*

Men on the march, Frank Brangwyn, 25" x 40", Pipes and Tobacco League, Avenue Press, London. $300-$400. *Courtesy of Swann Galleries.*

Keep these flags proudly flying, unsigned, 10" x 60", Parliamentary Recruiting Committee, No. 71B, Chorley and Pickersgill Ltd., Leeds, London. $100-$150.

Answer the call right quickly, unsigned, 10" x 60", Parliamentary Recruiting Committee, No. 71C, Chorley and Pickersgill, Ltd., Leeds, London. $100-$150.

Do your bit save food, Maurice Randall, 20" x 30", Hill, Sifkin and Co., London. $300-$400. *Courtesy of Swann Galleries.*

Daddy, what did you do in the Great War?, Saville Lumley, 20" x 30", Parliamentary Recruiting Committee, Johnson, Riddle and Co. London. $1500-$2000. A classic of the British war poster series, very scarce. *Courtesy of Swann Galleries.*

Put strength in the final blow, Frank Brangwyn, 40" x 60", War Bonds, Avenue Press London. $600-$750. Unusually graphic combat image by one of the greatest war artists.

Are you in this?, Lt. Gen. Sir R. S. S. Baden Powell, 20" x 30", Parliamentary Recruiting Committee, No. 112, Johnson Riddle and Co., London. $200-$300.

What in the end will settle this war?, unsigned, 10" x 30", Parliamentary Recruiting Committee, No. 66, Straker Brothers Ltd., London. $75-$100.

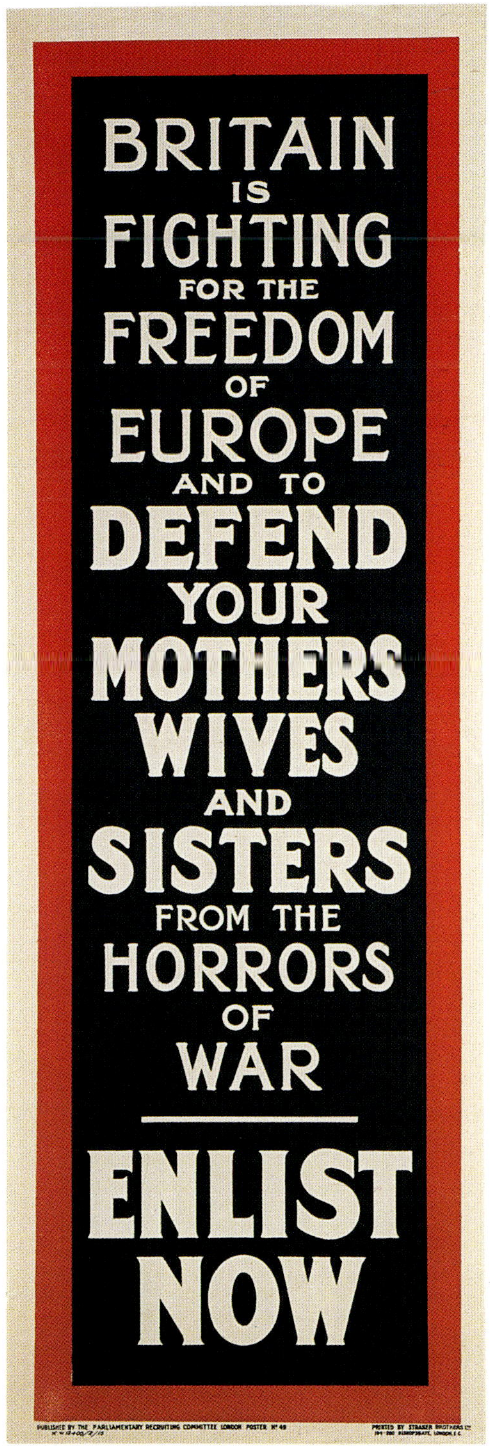

Britain is fighting for the freedom of Europe, unsigned, 10" x 30", Parliamentary Recruiting Committee, No. 49, Straker Brothers Ltd., London. $75-$100.

Fight for freedom with the strength of free men, unsigned, 10" x 30", Parliamentary Recruiting Committee, No. 48, Roberts and Leete Ltd., London. $50-$75.

What in the end will settle this war?, unsigned, 10" x 26", Parliamentary Recruiting Committee, No. 56, H. and C. Graham Ltd., London. $50-$75.

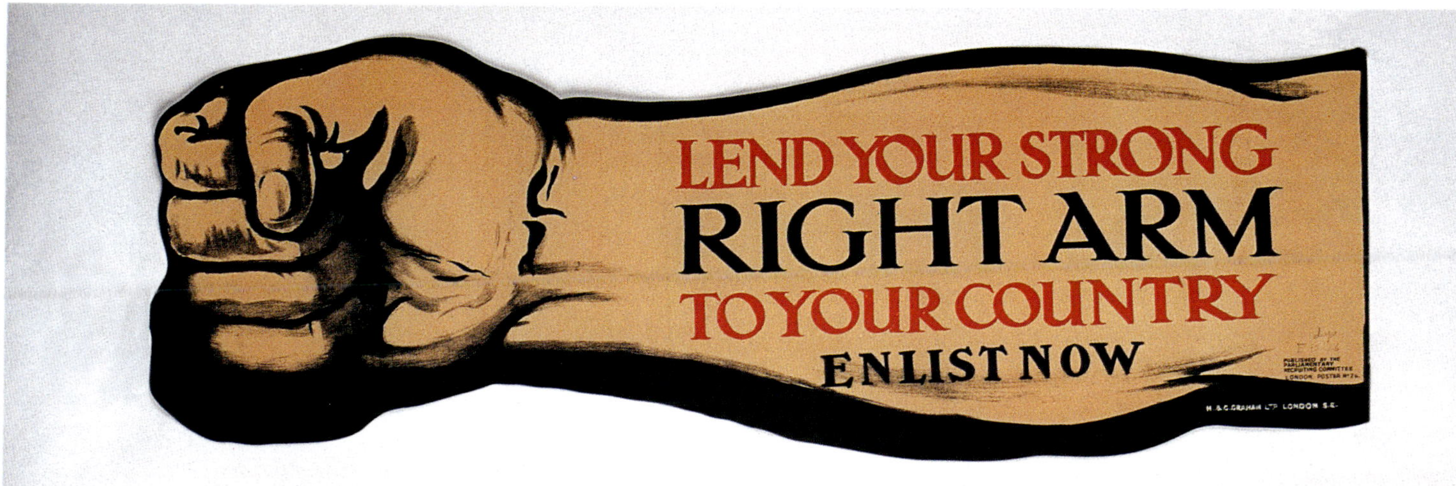

Lend your strong right arm, unsigned, die-cut 9" x 25", Parliamentary Recruiting Committee, No. 26, H. and C. Graham Ltd., London. $75-$100. Unusual die-cut poster, also exists in large format.

A call to arms, unsigned, 10" x 32", Parliamentary Recruiting Committee, No. 8, H. W. and V. Ltd. $50-$75.

In her hour of need, 10" x 32", Parliamentary Recruiting Committee, No. 9, H. W. and V. Ltd. $50-$75.

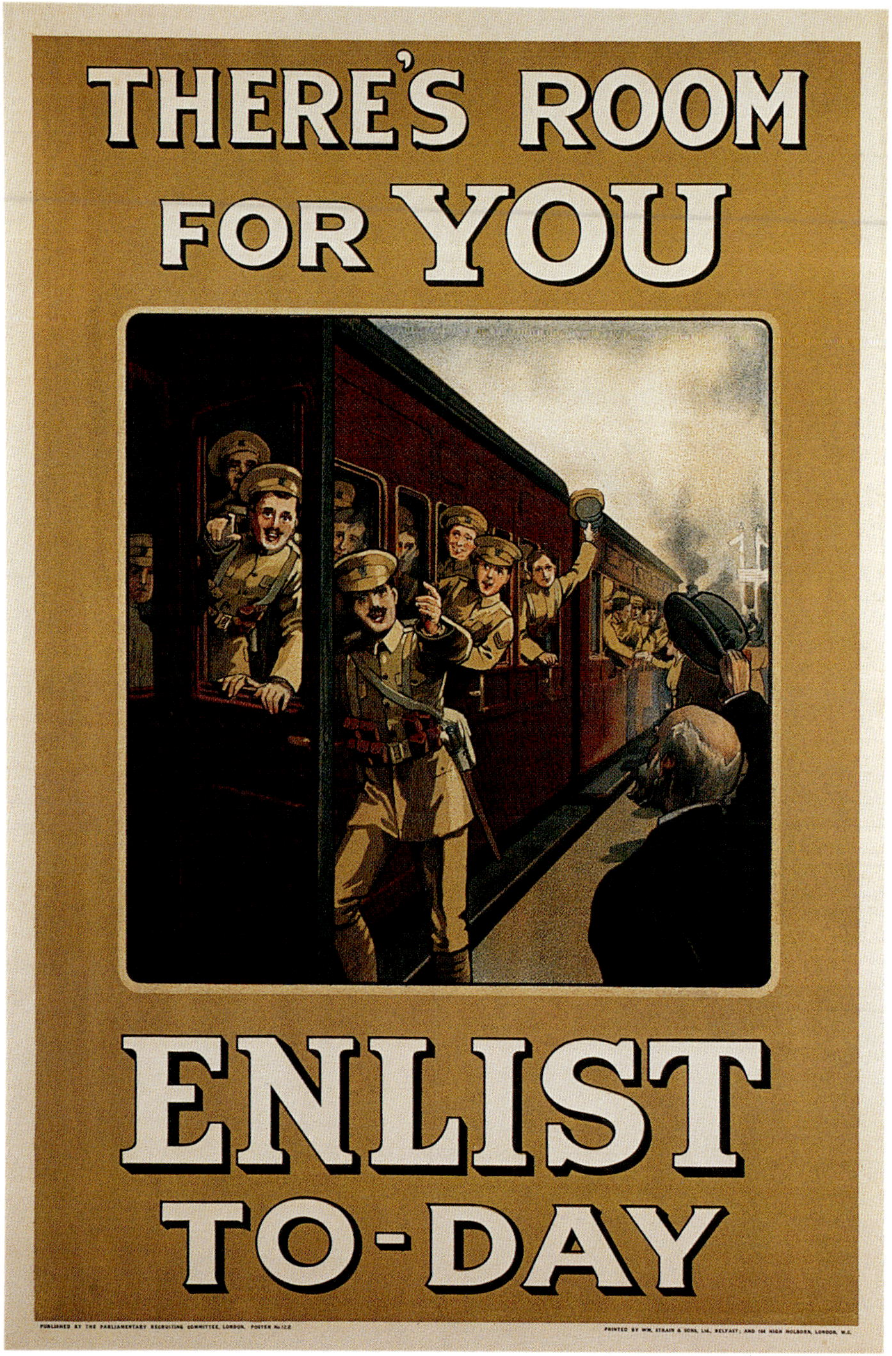

There's room for you, unclear signature, 20" x 30", Parliamentary Recruiting Committee, London, Poster No. 122, W. M. Strain and Sons Ltd., Belfast and London. $300-$450.

Women of Britain say - "Go!", unsigned, 20" x 30", Parliamentary Recruiting Committee, No. 75. Hill, Siffken and Co., London. $500-$650.

3 Questions to employers, unsigned, 20" x 30", Parliamentary Recruiting Committee, No. 70, Bemrose and Sons Ltd., London. $75-$100.

To the women of Britain, unsigned, 20" x 30", Parliamentary Recruiting Committee, No. 69, Bemrose and Sons Ltd., London. $75-$100.

The British sovereign will win, unsigned, 20" x 30", Parliamentary War Savings Committee, No. 9, David Allen and Sons Ltd, Harrow, Middlesex. $150-$200.

Remember Scarborough!, unsigned, 20" x 30", Parliamentary Recruiting Committee, No. 29, Harrison and Sons, London. $100-$150.

Remember Belgium, enlist today, unsigned, 15" x 20", Parliamentary Recruiting Committee, No. 19, Henry Jenkinson Ltd., Kirkstall, Leeds. $100-$150.

Single men, unsigned, 20" x 30", Parliamentary Recruiting Committee, No. 120, Abbey Press, London. $150-$200.

Come into the ranks and fight, unsigned, 25" x 38", Parliamentary Recruiting Committee, No. 74, Roberts and Leete Ltd., London. $300-$450.

Untitled, unsigned, 24" x 38", Parliamentary Recruiting Committee, No. 129, David Allen and Sons, Harrow, Middlesex. $300-$450. Remarkable recruiting poster without text, but the message is perfectly clear!

Mars appeals to Vulcan, Frank Brangwyn, 20" x 30", Daily Chronicle, Avenue Press Ltd., London. $300-$450.

The Zeppelin raids: the vow of vengeance, Frank Brangwyn, 20" x 30", The Daily Chronicle, Avenue Press Ltd., London. $300-$450.

Everyone should do his bit, Baron Low, 20" x 30", Parliamentary Recruiting Committee, London, No. 121, Roberts and Leete Ltd., London. $400-$550. Scarce poster showing Boy Scout and images of actual British war posters in background.

We're both needed to serve the guns!, unsigned, 40" x 50", Parliamentary Recruiting Committee, No. 85B, Chorley and Pickersgill Ltd., Leeds and London. $400-$550. Also seen in 20" x 30" format, value $200-$300.

Your country's call, unsigned, 20" x 30", Parliamentary Recruiting Committee. London, No. 87, Jowett and Sowry, Leeds. $300-$450.

(Welch) *Gymry sengl!*, unsigned, 15" x 20", Parliamentary and Joint Labour Recruiting Committees, No. 161, Roberts and Leete Ltd., London. $100-$150. Welsh posters are scarce!

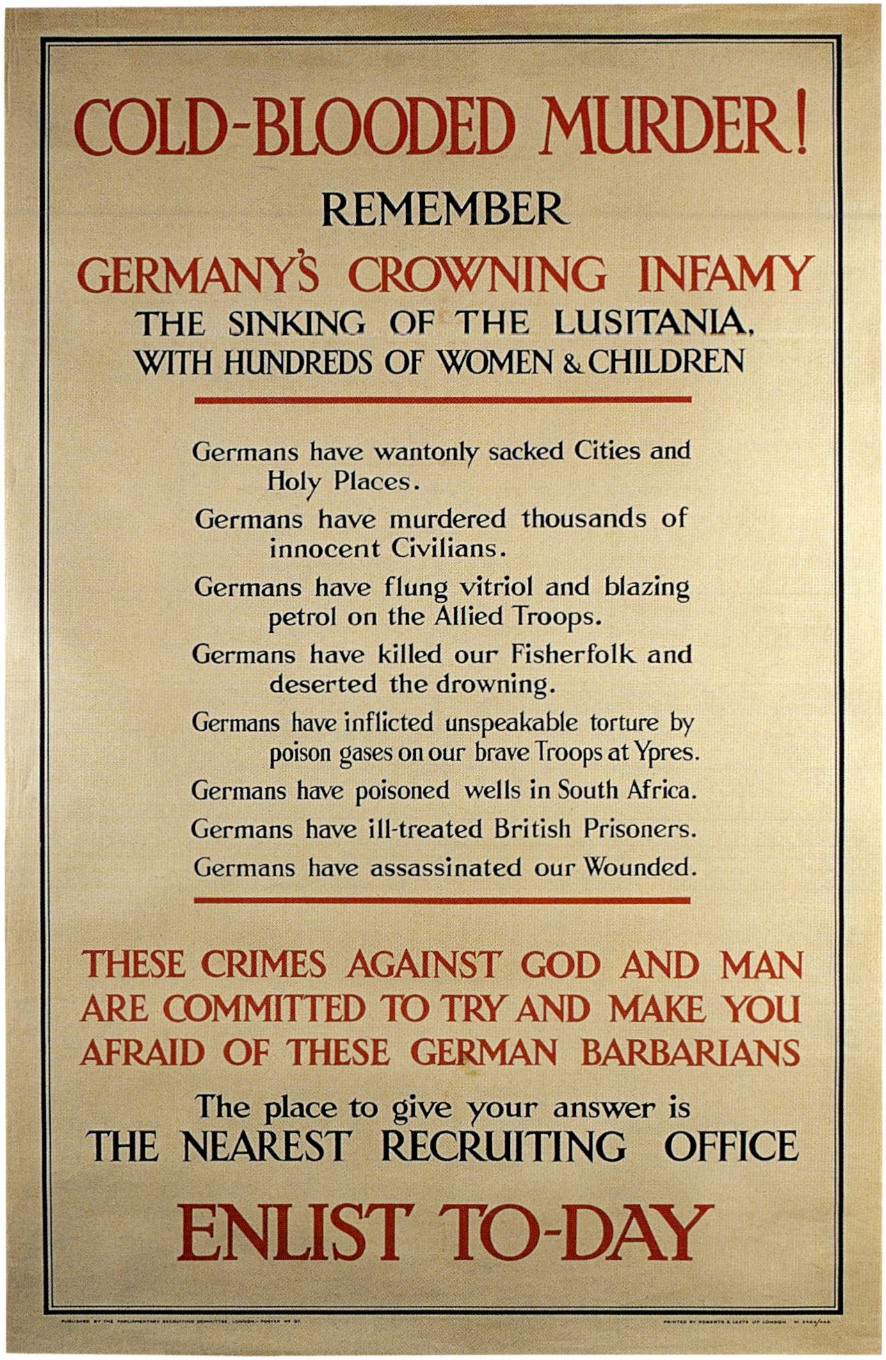

Cold-blooded murder!, unsigned, 25" x 40", Parliamentary Recruiting Committee, No. 97, Roberts and Leete Ltd., London. $100-$150.

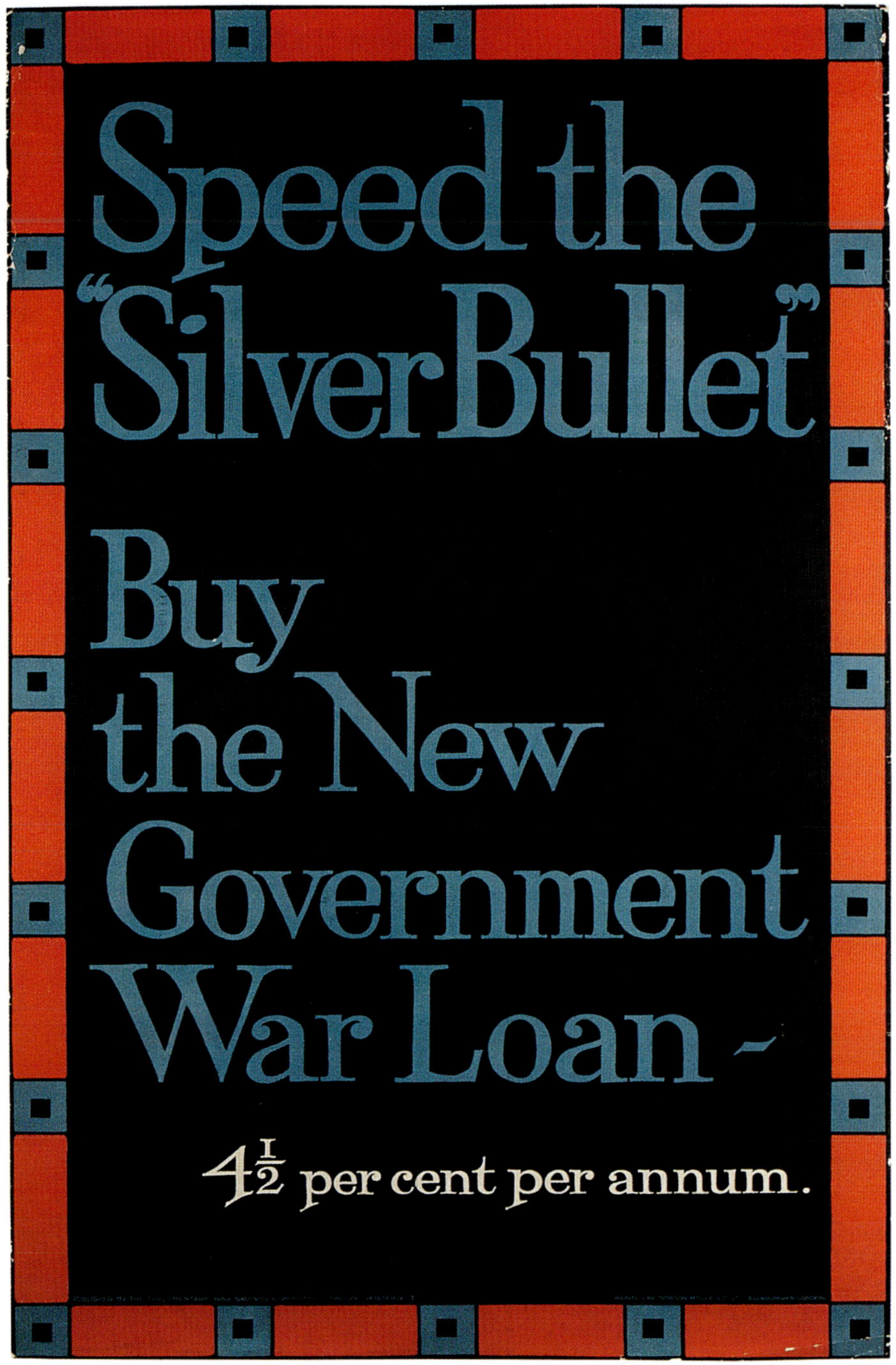

Speed the "silver bullet", unsigned, 25" x 40", Parliamentary War Savings Committee, No. 3, Dobson, Molle and Co. Ltd., Edinburgh and London. $100-$150.

Forward to victory, enlist now, unsigned, 20" x 30", Parliamentary Recruiting Committee, no printer. $400-$550. Also seen in 40" x 60" size, value $1500-$2000. Great imagery of charging cavalry officer, very scarce, especially in larger format.

Surely you will fight, unsigned, 20" x 30", Parliamentary Recruiting Committee, No. 83, Jas. Truscott and Son, London. $150-$200.

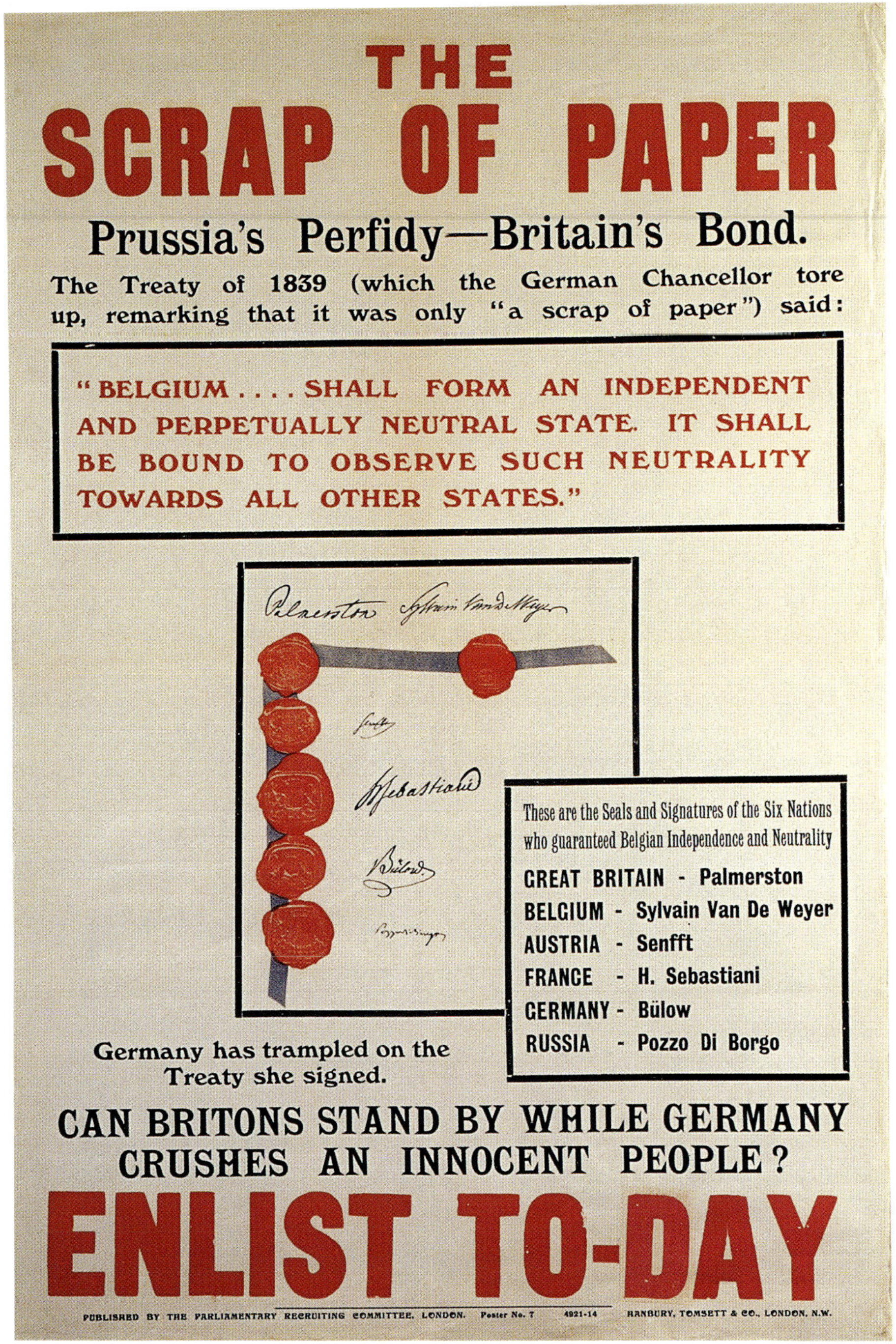

The scrap of paper, unsigned, 20" x 30", Parliamentary Recruiting Committee, No. 7, Hanbury, Tomsett and Co., London. $100-$150.

Why aren't you in khaki?, unsigned, 20" x 30", Parliamentary Recruiting Committee, No. 65, Jas. Truscott and Son, London. $100-$150.

Make us as proud of you as we are of him!, unsigned, Parliamentary Recruiting Committee, No. 119, David Allen and Sons Ltd., Harrow, Middlesex. $100-$150.

Which have you a reason or only an excuse?, unsigned, 20" x 30", Parliamentary Recruiting Committee, No. 128, Abbey Press, London. $100-$150.

The Prime Minister's pledge, unsigned, 20" x 30", Parliamentary Recruiting Committee No. 140, David Allen and Sons, Harrow, Middlesex. $75-$100.

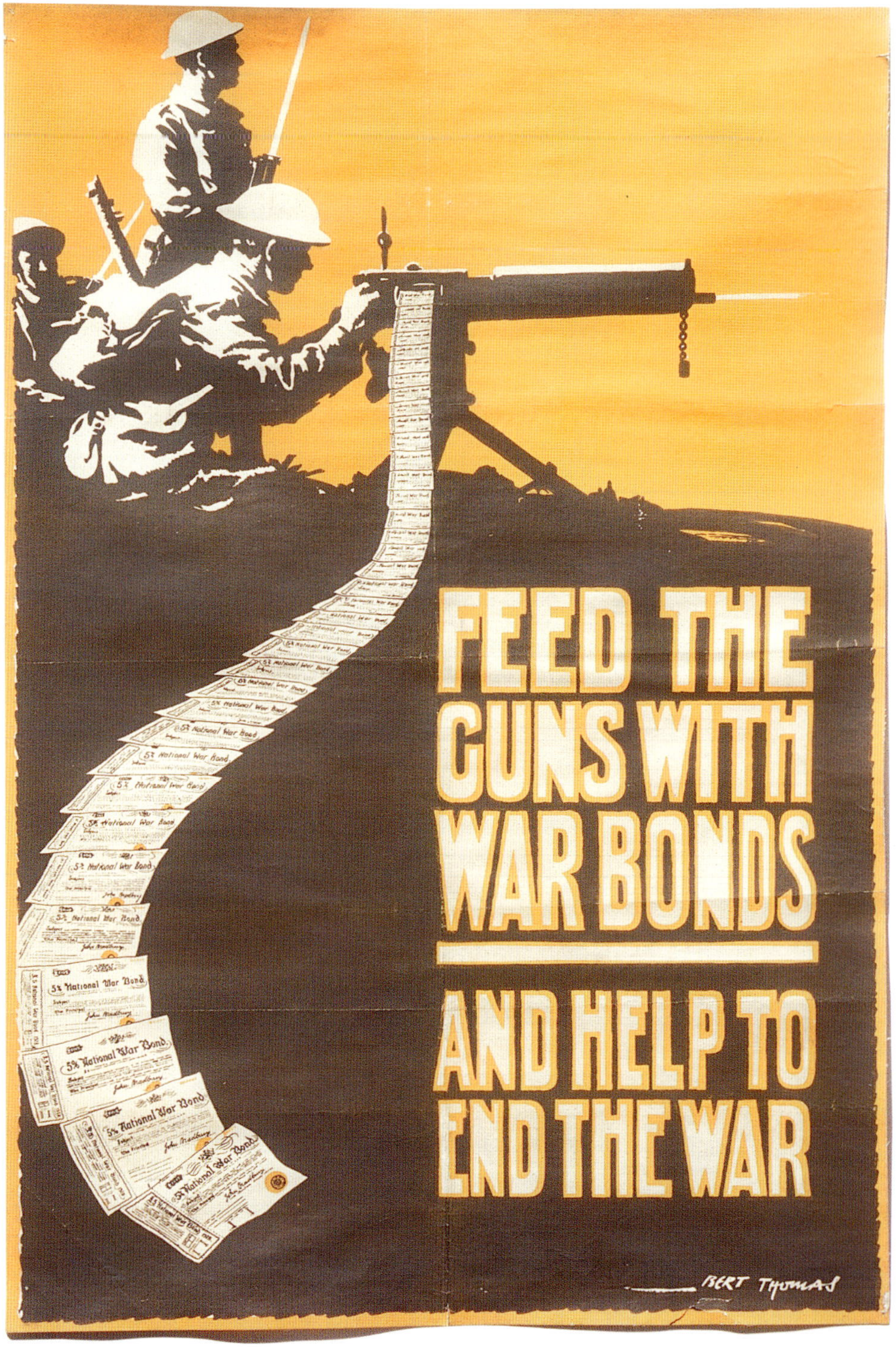

Feed the guns with war bonds, Bert Thomas, 19" x 28", War Bonds, no printer. $200-$300. *Courtesy of Robert Segel.*

Australia

(Australia) *"Well boy-you've done your bit"*, unsigned, 20" x 30", Australia Peace Bonds, E. B. Studios, Sydney. $750-$1000. Australian war posters are very uncommon. *Courtesy of Swann Galleries.*

France

Armee de Paris, unsigned, 19" x 24", Imprimerie Marcel Picard, Paris. $150-$200.

Souscrivez pour la victoire, Lucien Jonas, 31" x 47", 4e. Emprunt de la Defense National, Chacoin, Paris. $300-$450.

Debout dans la tranchee, Jean Droit, 31" x 45", 3e. Emprunt de la Defense Nationale, Devambez, Paris. $300-$450.

Opposite page: *4e. Emprunt de la Defense Nationale*, Jules Abel Faivre, 4e. Emprunt de la Defense Nationale, Devambez, Paris. $300-$450. *Courtesy of Swann Galleries.*

Emprunt National 1920, Castro, 24" x 31.5", Banque Nationale du Nord, Devambez, Paris. $150-$200.

Vous aussi faites votre devoir, B. Chavannez, 31" x 47", Credit Commerciale de France, Crete, Paris. $300-$450.

Pour que la France soit victorieuse, unclear signature, 32" x 44.5", 4e. Emprunt de la Defense Nationale, Devambez, Paris. $150-$200.

Pour que la France victorieuse comme a Valmy, A. Willette, 31.5" x 47", 4e. Emprunt National, Devambez, Paris. $200-$300.

Emprunt de la Paix, B. Chavannez, 31" x 47", Emprunt de la Paix, Crete, Paris. $300-$450.

3e. Emprunt de la Defense Nationale, unsigned, 31" x 47", 3e. Emprunt de la Defense Nationale, DeLong, Draeger. $300-$450.

Pour le dernier quart d'heure, S. E. M., 31" x 47", Banque Nationale du Credit, Devambez, Paris. $300-$450.

3e. Emprunt de la Defense Nationale, Auguste Leroux, 30.5" x 44", 3e. Emprunt de la Defense Nationale, Joseph Charles, Paris. $300-$450.

Opposite page: *Souscrivez pour hater la paix par la victoire*, 31.5" x 45", 3e. Emprunt de la Defense Nationale, Albert Besnard, Maquet Gr., Paris. $300-$450.

Pour le triomphe souscrivez a l'Emprunt Nationale, S. E. M., 31" x 45", Banque Nationale de Credit, Devambez, Paris. $300-$450.

3e. Emprunt de la Defense Nationale, Credit Lyonnaise, Abel Faivre, 22" x 31", Devambez, Paris. $200-$300. Also seen in 31" x 47" format, value $300-$450.

3e EMPRUNT
DEFENSE
ONALE
Besnard
1917
SOUSCRIVEZ
POUR HÂTER
LA PAIX
PAR
LA VICTOIRE
MAQUET Gr. PARIS.

Credit Lyonnaise Souscrivez au 4e. Emprunt Nationale, Abel Faivre, 22" x 31", 4e. Emprunt National, Devambez, Paris. $200-$300. Also seen in 31" x 47" format, value $300-$450.

Italy

Prestito Nazionale, Mario Borgoni, 40" x 51", Prestito Nazionale, Officine dell' Instituto Italiano d'Arti Grafiche, Bergamo. $500-$650. *Courtesy of Swann Galleries.*

Imitateli! Sottoscrivete al Prestito Nazionale 5%, Aldo Mazza, 39" x 60", Prestito Nazionale, no printer. $500-$650. *Courtesy of Swann Galleries.*

Prestito della Liberazione, Achille Mauzan, 40" x 56.5", Prestito della Liberazione, G. Ricordi, Milan. $750-$1000.

Per la liberazione, Achille Mauzan, 38" x 55", Prestito della Liberazione, G. Ricordi, Milan. $750-$1000. *Courtesy of Swann Galleries.*

Cacciali via!, Ugo Finozzi, 39" x 55", Prestito Nationale, R. & C. $600-$750. *Courtesy of Swann Galleries.*

Per la liberta e la civilta del mondo, Marcello Dudovich, 28" x 39", Prestito Nationale, Butteri, Torino. $600-$750.

Germany

Durch arbeit zum Zeig!, Alexander M. Cay, 25" x 38", A. Wohlfeld, Magdeburg. $500-$650. *Courtesy of Swann Galleries.*

Tonhalle Munchen, Ludwig Hohlwein, 17" x 24", Red Cross Soldier's Artwork Exhibition, Fritz Maison, Munchen. $900-$1200. *Courtesy of Swann Galleries.*

Ludendorf-spende, Ludwig Hohlwein, 23" x 34.5", Disabled Veterans Fund, Hollerbaum and Schmidt, Berlin. $900-$1200. *Courtesy of Swann Galleries.*

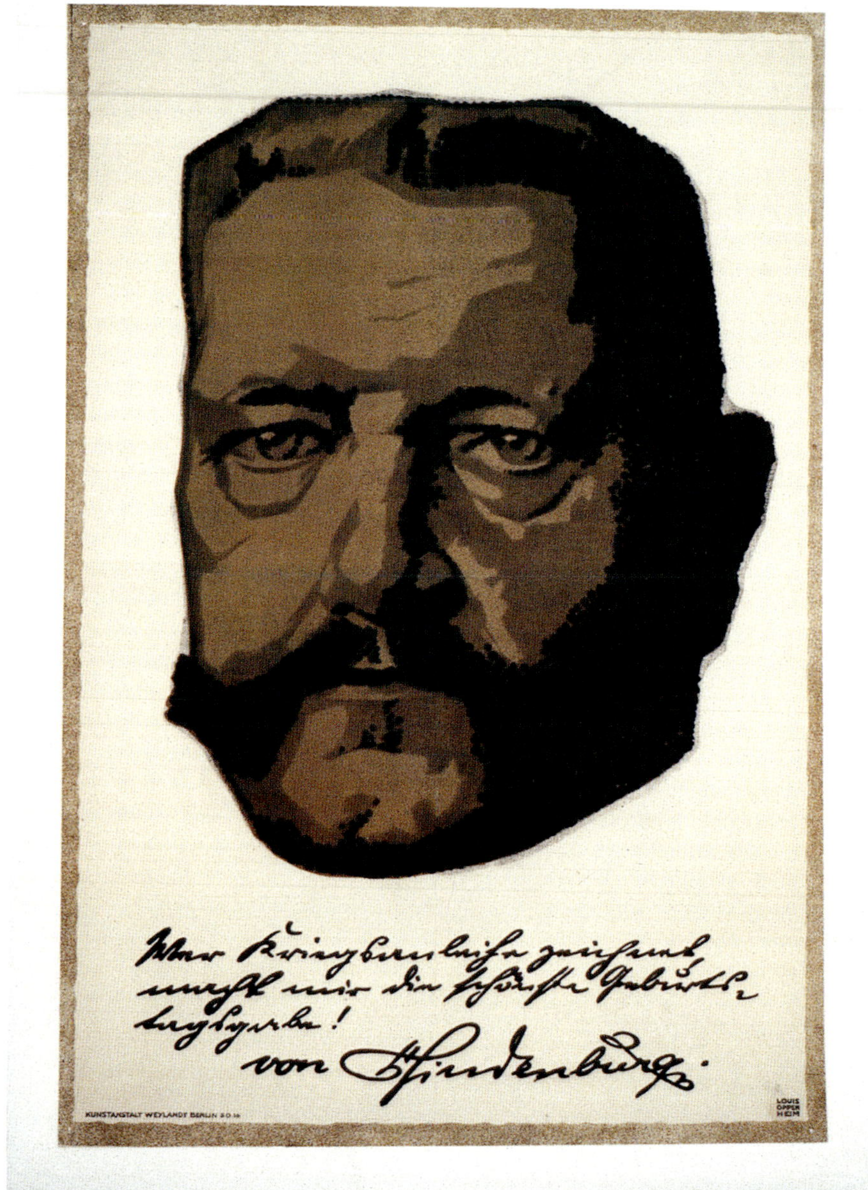

Volkspende, Ludwig Hohlwein, 22" x 34.5", Peoples Charity for German Prisoners of War, Hollerbaum and Schmid, Berlin. $900-$1200. *Courtesy of Swann Galleries.*

Von Hindenburg, Louis Oppenheim, 18.5" x 27", Weylandt, Berlin. $900-$1200. *Courtesy of Swann Galleries.*

Russia

(Russian) *5 1/2 % Military Loan*, Ivan A. Vladimirov, 27" x 39", Military Loan. $1000-$1250. Russian war posters are very scarce, this shows M1910 Maxim machine gun on Sokolov wheeled field mount. *Courtesy of Robert Segel.*

Bibliography

Creel, George. *How We Advertised America*. New York: Harper and Brothers, 1920.

Fusco, Tony. *The Official Identification and Price Guide to Posters*. New York: House of Collectibles, 1990.

Goodrum, Charles and Helen Dalrymple. *Advertising in America, The First 200 Years*. New York: Harry N. Abrams, Inc., 1990.

Hillier, Bevis. *Posters*. New York: Stein and Day, 1969.

Johnson, J. Stewart. *The Modern American Poster*. Boston: Little, Brown and Co., 1983.

Kiehl, David W. *American Art Posters of the 1890s*. New York: The Metropolitan Museum of Art, 1987.

Mock, James R., and Cedric Larson. *Words That Won the War: The Story of the Committee on Public Information, 1917-1919*. Princeton, New Jersey: Princeton University Press, 1939.

Pennell, Joseph. *Joseph Pennell's Liberty-Loan Poster: A Textbook for Artists and Amateurs, Governments and Teachers and Printers*. Philadelphia: J. B. Lippincott, 1918.

Rawls, Walton. *Wake Up, America! World War I and the American Poster*. New York: Abbeville Press, 1988.

Reed, Walt. *The Illustrator in America 1900-1960s*. New York: Reinhold Publishing Co., 1966.

Richmond, Leonard. *The Technique of the Poster*. London: Sir Isaac Pittman and Sons, Ltd., 1933.

Rickards, Maurice. *Posters of the First World War*. New York: Walker and Co., 1968.

Theofiles, George. *American Posters of World War I*. New York: Dafran House Publishers, 1973.